Richard Johnson

A New History of the Grecian States

From their earliest period to their extinction by the Ottomans; containing an account of their most memorable sieges and battles

Richard Johnson

A New History of the Grecian States
From their earliest period to their extinction by the Ottomans; containing an account of their most memorable sieges and battles

ISBN/EAN: 9783337093686

Printed in Europe, USA, Canada, Australia, Japan

Cover: Foto ©ninafisch / pixelio.de

More available books at **www.hansebooks.com**

FRONTISPIECE

Fame crowning with Laurel the Historian
Xenophon who is supported by Poetry
& Oratory

A NEW HISTORY OF THE GRECIAN STATES;

FROM

Their earliest Period to their Extinction by the OTTOMANS.

CONTAINING

AN ACCOUNT

OF THEIR MOST

MEMORABLE SIEGES AND BATTLES;

AND

THE CHARACTER AND EXPLOITS

OF THEIR MOST CELEBRATED

HEROES, ORATORS, AND PHILOSOPHERS.

EMBELLISHED WITH COPPER-PLATE CUTS.

DESIGNED FOR THE USE OF
YOUNG LADIES AND GENTLEMEN.

LONDON, PRINTED :
LANSINGBURGH, *(New-York)*,
RE-PRINTED BY *SILVESTER TIFFANY*, for,
and sold by, THOMAS SPENCER, at his
Book-Store, Market-street, *Albany*,
M DCC XCIV.

PREFACE.

THE very flattering Reception my *History of the Roman Commonwealth* has received, has encournged me to attempt, on the same plan, and with the same views, A History of the Grecian States: those States which, though inconsiderable in their extent, gave law to the surrounding nations, and brought savage man, who till then wandered in the wilds of ignorance and barbarity, into the pale of civil society, and forced the rude customs of savages to yield to the refinements of the polite arts and sciences. Though her lofty domes are now no longer visible, though her stately and magnificent cities have been long since levelled with the earth, and the martial spirit has ceased to exist on Grecian soil; yet the deeds of her Heroes, Legislators, and Philosophers, will die only with Time itself.

After what has been advanced in the Preface to my Roman History, little need further be said in apology for this publication. I shall, therefore, only just mention the three heroes of my Frontispiece.

HOMER was the most celebrated and illustrious of all the Poets of antiquity; and yet we are not certain of what part of Greece he was a native; nor do we know exactly the time of his birth, though he is generally supposed to have lived about eight hundred and forty years before Christ. No nation in the world has produced poems comparable to his.

XENOPHON

PREFACE.

Xenophon was so celebrated a Greek Historian, that they called him the *Attic Bee*. He was a scholar of Socrates, and no less the warrior than the scholar. He wrote several books, of which some are still in being, and their stile is considered as a master piece. His Cyropædia, which he dedicated to Cyrus, has not its equal.

The character of Demosthenes, the most celebrated Athenian Orator, will be found in different parts of this work. We have here only to add, that, when Antipater succeeded Alexander, he fled to save his life; and, in order to avoid falling into his enemy's hands, he swallowed poison, which he had prepared and kept for that purpose in his pen, and so ended his days.

CONTENTS.

CONTENTS.

CHAP. I.
A view of the earliest State of Greece —The Laws of Lycurgus—The Death of that great Legislator - - Page 9

CHAP. II.
The Athenians appoint Draco their Law-maker He is succeeded by Solon—Salamis taken—The Seven Wise Men—The Areopagus, and Council of Four Hundred—Pisistratus usurps the Government of Athens—the Death of Solon - - - Page 19

CHAP. III.
Character of Aristides and Themistocles—Battle of Marathon—Singular Bravery of Cyndærus—The Persians make an ineffectual Attempt to surprize Athens—Honours paid to Miltiades—Death of that brave General—Piety of his Son Cimon - Page 26

CHAP. IV.
Xerxes sets out for the Conquest of Greece—His Vanity and Presumption—His immense Army—Builds a Bridge across the Hellespont—Lands in Europe and marches into Greece—The Lacedemonians wait for him at the Straits of Thermopylæ—Noble Death of Leonidas and his Followers—The Greeks gain an Advantage over the Persian Fleet—

Athens *taken and demolished*—*Battle* of Salamis—Xerxes *retreats disgracefully from* Greece - - - Page 34

CHAP. V.

Mardonius, *the* Persian *General defeated and killed*—*The* Persians *finally quit* Greece—*Character of* Aristides—*A terrible Plague breaks out at* Athens—*Character of* Pericles—*He changes the Government of* Athens *into a Kind of Monarchy*—*Death of* Pericles—*Character of* Alcibiades—*His Death*—*Character of* Socrates—*His Speech against the Accusations of* Melitus—*Death of* Socrates—*Veneration paid to his Memory* Page 45

CHAP. VI.

Agesilaus *chosen King of* Sparta—*Defeats the* Persians—Sparta *takes the Lead of* Athens—*The* Thebans *take the Lead of the* Spartans—*Character of* Epimanondas—*Battle of* Leuctra—*Celebrated Battle of* Mantinea—*Death of* Epimanondas - - Page 68

CHAP. VII.

First rise of Macedonia *from Obscurity*—Philip *institutes the* Macedonian *Phalanx*—*The Birth and Education of* Alexander—Philip *loses one of his Eyes*—Demosthenes *warns the* Athenians *of their Danger*—*Singular Instance of Ingratitude*—Alexander *saves the Life of his Father* Philip—*Battle of* Chæronea—Demosthenes *flies from the Field of Battle—Death of* Philip - - Page 81

CHAP. VIII.

Alexander *succeeds his Father* Philip—*Takes the City of* Thebes, *and plunders it—Appointed Generalissimo against the* Persians—*Lands in* Asia *without Opposition—Battle on the Banks of the* Grannicus—*Takes several Places —Cuts the* Gordian *Knot—Magnificence and Pomp of the Army of* Darius - Page 96

CHAP. IX.

Darius *defeated at the Battle of* Issus—*His Mother, Wife, and Children, taken Prisoners—* Alexander *treats them with great Honour and Generosity—*Abdalonymus *made King of the* Sidonians—*The City of* Tyre *taken by storm* Page 107

CHAP. X.

Alexander *refuses Overtures of Peace made by* Darius—Alexander's *Cruelty at* Gaza—*Death of* Statira, Darius's *Queen—Battle of* Arbela—Alexander *enters* Babylon, *and then* Persepolis—*Death of* Darius - Page 114

CHAP. XI.

Alexander *pursues his Conquests—Abandons himself to Sensuality—Puts some of his old Friends to Death—Kills* Clytus—*Is exposed to great Danger of his Life in* India—*Sets out on his Return*

CONTENTS.

Return to Babylon—His Death - Page 113

CHAP. XII.

From the Death of Alexander, to the Extinction of the Grecian States by the Ottomans Page 130

Chronological Table of the principal Occurrences and Events during the Existence of the Grecian States - - Page 141

THE HISTORY OF THE GRECIAN STATES.

CHAP. I.

GREECE, in its earliest infancy, was a combination of little states, each governed by its respective sovereign, yet all uniting for their mutual safety and general advantage. Their intestine contentions, however, were carried on with great animosity; and, as it happens in all petty states under the dominion of a single commander, the jealousies of the princes were a continual cause of discord. From this distressful situation, those states, by degrees, began to emerge; a different spirit began to seize the people, and, sick of the contentions of their princes, they desired to be free. A spirit of liberty prevailed all over Greece, and a general change of government was effected in every part of the country, except in Macedonia. Thus monarchy gave way to a republican government, which, however, was diversified into as many various forms as there were different cities, according to the peculiar character of each people.

Though

Though these cities seemed to differ from each other in their laws and interests, yet they were united by one common language, one religion, and a national pride, that taught them even to consider all other nations as barbarous and feeble. Even Egypt itself, from whence they had derived many of their arts and institutions, was considered in a very subordinate light. To make this union among the states of Greece still stronger, there were games instituted in different parts of the country, with rewards for excellence in every pursuit. These sports were instituted for very serious and useful purposes: they afforded an opportunity for the several states meeting together; they gave them a greater zeal for their common religion; they exercised the youths for the purposes of war, and encreased that vigour and activity, which were then of the utmost importance in deciding the fate of a battle.

Their chief bond of union, however, arose from the council of the Amphictyons, which was instituted by Amphictyon, king of Athens, about the year 2500, and was appointed to be held twice a year at Thermopylee, to deliberate for the general good of those states, of whose deputies it was composed. The states, who sent deputies to this council, were twelve, namely, the Thessalians, the Thebans, the Dorians, the Ionians, the Perhaabeans, the Magnates, the Locrians, the Oetans, the Pthiotes, the Maleans, the Phocians, and the Delopians. Each of these cities, which had a right to assist at the Amphictyonic council, was obliged

to

to send two deputies to every meeting. The one was entitled the Hieromnemon, who took care of the interests of religion; the other was called the Pylagoras, and had in charge the civil interests of his community.

This confederacy united the Greeks for a time into a body of great power, and greater emulation. By this association, a country, not half so large as England, was able to dispute the empire of the earth with the most powerful monarchs of the world; by this association, they not only made head against the numerous armies of Persia, but dispersed, routed, and destroyed them, reducing their pride so low, as to make them submit to conditions of peace, as shameful to the conquered as glorious to the conquerors. But, among all the cities of Greece there were two, which by their merit, their valour, and their wisdom, particularly distinguished themselves from the rest: these were Athens and Lacedæmon. As these cities served for examples of bravery or learning to the rest, and as the chief burthen of every foreign war devolved upon them, we shall proceed to give the reader a general idea of the genius, character, manners, and government, of their respective inhabitants.

Though the kingdom of Lacedæmon was not so considerable as that of Athens, yet, as it was of much earlier institution, it deserves our first attention. Lacedæmon was, for a long time, governed with turbulence and oppression, and required the curb of severe laws and rigorous discipline. These severities and rigorous discipline were at laſt impoſed upon it by Licurgus, one of the firſt and moſt extraordinary legiſlators that ever appeared among mankind. There is perhaps nothing more remarkable in profane hiſtory, yet nothing ſo well atteſted, as what relates to the laws and government of Lycurgus. What indeed can be more amazing, than to behold a mutinous and ſavage race of mankind yielding ſubmiſſion to laws, that controuled every ſenſual pleaſure, and every private affection! To behold them give up for the good of the ſtate, all the comforts and conveniences of private life, and making a ſtate of domeſtic privacy more ſevere and terrible, than the moſt painful campaigns and the moſt warlike duties! Yet all this was effected by the perſeverance and authority of a ſingle legiſlator, who gave the firſt leſſons of hard reſignation in his own generous examples.

Lycurgus was the ſon of Eunomus, one of the two kings who reigned together in Sparta: During the minority of Charilaus, Licurgus acted as regent; but reſolving to make himſelf acquainted with all the improvements of other nations, he travelled into Crete, paſſed over into Aſia, and from thence went into Egypt. But while he was thus employed abroad, his preſence was greatly wanted at home, where every thing was haſtening to anarchy and ruin. On his return, he found the people wearied out with their own importunities, and ready to receive any new impreſſions he might attempt. He firſt communicated his deſign of

altering

altering the whole code of laws to his particular friends, and then by degrees gained over the leading men to his party, until things being ripe for a change, he ordered thirty of the principal men to appear armed in the market-place. Charilus, who was at this time king, at first opposed the revolution, but was soon persuaded to join in the measure.

To continue the kings still with a shadow of power, he confirmed them in their rights of succession as before; but diminished their authority by instituting a senate, which was to serve as a counterpoise between the prerogative and the people. The kings however, had still all their former marks of outward dignity and respect. The government hitherto had been unsteady, tending at one time towards despotism, at another to democracy; but the senate instituted by Lycurgus served as a check upon both, and kept the state balanced in tranquility.

To keep the people in plenty and dependence, seems to have been one of the most refined strokes in this philosopher's legislation. The generality of people were at that time so poor, that they were destitute of every kind of possession, while a small number of individuals were possessed of all the lands and the wealth of the country. In order, therefore, to banish the insolence, the fraud, and the luxury of the one, as well as the misery, the repining, and the factious despair of the other, he persuaded the majority, and forced the rest, to give up all their lands to the commonwealth, and to make a new division of them, that they might all live together in perfect equality. Thus all the sensual goods of life were distributed among the governors and the governed, and superior merit alone conferred superior distinction.

It would, however, have answered no permanent purpose to divide the lands, if the money had been still suffered to accumulate. To prevent, therefore, all other distinctions but that of merit, he resolved to level down all fortune to one standard. He did not, indeed, strip those possessed of gold or silver of their property; but, what was equivalent, he cried down its value, and suffered nothing but iron money to pass in exchange for every commodity. This coin also he made so heavy, and fixed at so low a rate, that a cart and two oxen were required to carry home a sum equivalent to twenty pounds English, and a whole house was necessary to keep it in. By these means, money was soon brought into disuse, and few troubled themselves with more than was sufficient to supply their necessaries. Thus not only riches, but their attendant train of avarice, fraud, rapine, and luxury, were banished from this simple state.

Even these institutions were not thought sufficient to prevent that tendency, which mankind have to private excess. A third regulation was therefore made, commanding that all meals should be in public. He ordained, that all the men should eat in one common hall without distinction; and, lest strangers should attempt to corrupt his citizens by their examples, a law was expressly made against their entrance into the city. By these means, frugality was not only made necessary, but the use of riches was at once abolished. Every man sent monthly his provisions to the common stock, with a little money for other contingent expences.

So rigorous an injunction, which thus cut off all the delicacies and refinements of luxury, was by no means pleasing to the rich, who took every occasion to insult the lawgiver on his new regulations. The tumults it excited were frequent; and in one of these, a young fellow, whose name was Alexander, struck out one of Lycurgus's eyes; but he had the majority of the people on his side, who, provoked at the outrage, delivered the young man into his hands, to treat him with all proper severity. Lycurgus, instead of testifying any brutal resentment, won over his aggressor by all the arts of ability and tenderness, till at last, from being one of the proudest and most turbulent men of Sparta, he became an example of wisdom and moderation, and an useful assistant to Lycurgus in promoting his new institutions.

Thus undaunted by opposition, and steady in his designs, he went on to make reformation in the manners of his countrymen. As the education of youth was one of the most important objects of a legislator's care, he first instituted, that such children as, upon a public view were deemed deformed or weekly, and unfitted for a future life of vigour and fatigue,

tigue, should be exposed to perish in a cavern near mount Taygetus. Those infants that were born without any capital defects, were adopted as children of the state, and delivered to their parents to be nursed with severity and hardship. From their tenderest age, they were accustomed to make no choice in their eating, nor to be afraid in the dark, or when left alone; not to be peevish or fretful, to walk barefoot, to lie hard at nights, to wear the same cloathes winter and summer, and to fear nothing from their equals. At the age of seven they were taken from their parents, and delivered over to the classes for their education. Their discipline there was little else than an apprenticeship to hardship, self-denial, and obedience.

All ostentatious learning was banished from this simple commonwealth: their only study was to obey, their only pride was to suffer hardships. There was yearly a custom of whipping them at the altar of Diana, and the boy that bore this punishment with the greatest fortitude came off victorious. Every institution seemed calculated to harden the body, and sharpen the mind for war. In order to prepare them for stratagems and sudden incursions, the boys were permitted to steal from each other; but, if they were caught in the fact, they were punished for their want of dexterity.

At twelve years old, the boys were removed into another class of a more advanced kind. There, in order to crush the seeds of vice
which,

which at that time began to appear, their labour and discipline were encreased with their age. They had now their skirmishes between parties, and their mock fights between larger bodies. In these they often fought with hands, feet, teeth, and nails with such obstinacy, that it was common to see them lose their eyes, and often their lives, before the fray was determined. Such was the constant discipline of their minority, which lasted till the age of thirty, before which they were not permitted to marry, to go into the troops, or to bear any office in the state.

With regard to the virgins, their discipline was equally strict with the former. They were inured to a constant course of labour and industry, until they were twenty years old, before which time they were not allowed to be marriageable.

Valour and generosity seemed the ruling motives of this new institution; arms were their only exercise and employment, and their life was much less austere in the camp than in the city. The Spartans were the only people in the world, to whom the time of war was a time of ease and refreshment; because then the severity of their manners was relaxed, and the men were indulged in greater liberties. With them the first principles of war was never to turn their backs on their enemies, however disproportioned in forces, nor to deliver up their arms until they resigned them with life.

Such was the general purport of the institutions of Lycurgus, which from their tendency gained the esteem and admiration of all the surrounding nations. The Greeks were ever apt to be dazzled rather with splendid than useful virtues, and praised the laws of Lycurgus, which at best were calculated rather to make men warlike than happy, and to substitute insensibility instead of enjoyment.

When Lycurgus had thus compleated his military institution, and when the form of government he had established seemed strong and vigorous enough to support itself, his next care was to give it all the permanence in his power. He therefore signified to the people, that something still remained for the completion of his plan, and that he was under the necessity of going to consult the oracle of Delphos for its advice. In the mean time, he persuaded them to take an oath, for the strict observance of all his laws until his return, and then departed with a full resolution of never seeing Sparta more. When he was arrived at Delphos, he consulted the oracle, to know whether the laws he had made were sufficient to render the Lacedæmonians happy; and being answered, that nothing was wanting to their perfection, he sent this answer to Sparta, and then voluntarily starved himself to death. Others say he died in Crete, ordering his body to be burnt, and his ashes to be thrown into the sea. The death of this great lawgiver gave a sanction and authority to his laws, which his life was unable to confer. The Spartans regarded his end as the most glorious of all his actions, and a noble finishing of all his former services. They built a temple, and paid divine honours to him after his death; they considered themselves as bound by every tie of gratitude and religion to a strict observance of all his institutions; and the long continuance of the Spartan government is a proof of their persevering resolution.

CHAP. II.

THE Athenians having, for more than a century, seen the good effects of laws in the regulation of the Spartan commonwealth, about the year 3380, became desirous of being governed by written laws. They pitched upon Draco, a man of acknowledged wisdom and unshaken integrity, but rigid even beyond human sufferance. Draco not succeeding in this business, Solon was applied to for his advice and assistance, as he was the wisest and justest man in all Athens. His great learning had acquired him the reputation of being the first of the seven wise men of Greece, and his known humanity procured him the love and veneration of every rank among his fellow citizens. Solon was a native of Salamis, an island dependent on Athens, but which had revolted to put itself under the power of the Megareans. In attempting to recover this island, the Athenians had spent much blood and treasure, until at last wearied out with such ill-success, a law was made, rendering it

capital

capital ever to advise the recovery of their lost possession. Solon, however, undertook to pusuade them to another trial; and, feigning himself mad, he ran about the streets, using the most violent gestures and language; but the purport of all was, to upbraid the Athenians for their remissness and effeminacy, in giving up their conquests in despair. In short, he acted his part so well, by the oddity of his manners, and the strength of his reasoning, that the people resolved on another expedition against Salamais; and, by a stratagem of his contrivance, in which he introduced several young men upon the island in women's cloaths, the place was surprised, and added to the dominion of Athens.

But this was not the only occasion, on which he exhibited superior address and wisdom. At a time when Greece had carried the arts of eloquence, poetry, and government, higher than they had yet been seen among mankind, Solon was considered as one of the foremost in each perfection. The sages of Greece, whose fame is still undiminished, acknowledged his merit, and adopted him as their associate. The correspondence between these wise men was at once instructive, friendly, and sincere. They were seven in number, namely, Thales the Milesian, Solon of Athens, Chilo of Lacedæmon, Pittacus of Mitylene, Periander of Corinth, Bias and Cleobulus, whose birth-places are not ascertained.

These sages often visited each other, and their conversations generally turned upon the methods of instituting the best form of government, or the arts of private happiness. One day, when Solon went to Miletus to see Thales, the first thing he said, was to express his surprise that Thales had never desired to marry, or have children. Thales made no answer then, but a few days after contrived that a stranger, supposed to arrive from Athens, should join their company. Solon, hearing from whence the stranger came, was inquisitive after the news of his own city, but was only informed, that a young man died there, for whom the whole place was in the greatest affliction, as he was reputed the most promising youth in all Athens. "Alas! (cried Solon) how much is the poor father of the youth to be pitied! Pray, what was his name?" "I heard the name, (replied the stranger, who was instructed for the occasion) but I have forgotten it: I only remember, that all people talked much of his wisdom and justice." Every answer afforded new matter of trouble and terror to the inquisitive father, and he had just strength enough to ask, if the youth was the son of Solon. "The very same," replied the stranger; at which words Solon shewed all the marks of the most inconsolable distress. This was the opportunity which Thales wanted, who took him by the hand, and said to him with a smile, "Comfort yourself, my friend, all that has been told you is a mere fiction, but may serve as a very proper answer to your question, why I never thought proper to marry."

One day, at the court of Periander of Corinth,

rinth, a question was proposed, "Which was the most perfect popular government?" "That (said Bias) where the laws have no superior." "That (said Thales) where the inhabitants are neither too rich nor too poor." "That (said Anacharsis the Scythian) where virtue is honoured and vice detested." "That (said Pittacus) where dignities are always conferred upon the virtuous, and never upon the base." "That (said Cleobulus) where the citizens fear blame more than punishment." "That (said Chilo) where the laws are more regarded than the orators." But Solon's opinion seems to have the greatest weight, who said, "Where an injury done to the meanest subject is an insult upon the whole constitution."

Upon a certain occasion, when Solon was conversing with Anacharsis, the Scythian philosopher, about his intended reformation in the state, "Alas (cried the Scythian) all your laws will be found to resemble spiders webs: the weak and small flies will be caught and entangled, but the great and powerful will always have strength enough to break through."

A matter still more celebrated is Solon's interview with Crœsus, king of Lydia. This monarch, who was reputed the richest of all Asia Minor, was willing to make an ostentatious display of his wealth before the Greek philosopher, and after shewing him immense heaps of treasures, and the greatest variety of other ornaments, he demanded, whether he did not think the possessor of them the most happy of all mankind. "No, (replied Solon) I know one more happy, a poor peasant of Greece, who, neither in affluence nor in poverty, has but few wants, and has learned to supply them by his labour." This answer was by no means agreeable to the vain monarch, who by this question hoped only for a reply that would tend to flatter his pride. Willing, therefore, to extort one still more favourable, he asked, whether, at least, he did not think him happy. "Alas! (cried Solon) what man can be pronounced happy before he dies!" The integrity and the wisdom of Solon's replies appeared in the event. The kingdom of Lydia was invaded by Cyrus, the empire destroyed, and Crœsus himself was taken prisoner. When he was led out to execution, according to the barbarous manner of the times, he then too late recollected the maxims of Solon, and could not help crying out when on the scaffold upon Solon's name. Cyrus, hearing him repeat the name with great earnestness, was desirous of knowing the reason; and being informed by Crœsus of that philosopher's remarkable observation, he began to fear for himself, pardoned Crœsus, and took him for the future into confidence and friendship. Thus Solon had the merit of saving one king's life, and of reforming another.

Such was the man, to whom Athens applied for assistance in reforming the severity of their government, and instituting a just body of law. His first attempt was, therefore, in favour of the poor, whose debts he abolished at once, by an exprefs law of infolvency. His next ftep was to repeal all the laws enacted by Draco, except thofe againft murder. He then proceeded to the regulation of offices, employments, and magiftrates, all which he left in the hands of the rich ; and he diftributed the rich into three claffes, ranging them according to their incomes. The Areopagus, fo called from the place where the court was held, had been eftablifhed fome centuries before, but Solon reftored and augmented its authority. Nothing was fo auguft as this court, and its reputation for judgment and integrity became fo very great, that the Romans fometimes referred caufes, which were too intricate for their own decifion, to the determination of this tribunal. Nothing was regarded here but truth : that no external objects might pervert juftice, the tribunal was held in darknefs, and the advocates were denied all attempts to work upon the paffions of the judges. Superior to this, Solon inftituted the great council of four hundred, who were to judge upon appeals from the Areopagus, and maturely to examine every queftion before it came to be debated in a general affembly of the people.

He abolifhed the cuftom of giving portions in marriage with young women, unlefs they were only daughters. The bride was to carry no other fortune to her hufband than three fuits of clothes, and fome houfehold goods of little value. It was his aim to prevent making matrimony a traffic : he confidered it as an honourable connection, calculated for the mutual happinefs hapiness of both parties, and the general advantage of the state.

These were the principal institutions of this celebrated lawgiver, and though neither so striking, nor yet so well authorised as those of Lycurgus, they did not fail to operate for several succeeding ages, and seemed to gather strength by observance. In order to perpetuate his statutes, he engaged the people by a public oath to observe them religiously, at least for the term of an hundred years: and thus, having completed the task assigned him, he withdrew from the city, to avoid the importunity of some, and the captious petulence of others; for, as he well knew, it was hard, if not impossible, to please every individual. Solon being now employed on his travels in visiting Egypt, Lydia, and several other countries, left Athens to become habituated to his new institutions, and to try by experience the wisdom of their formation.

While Solon was thus on his travels, civil contensions disturbed Athens, and the spirit of party was hastening every thing to ruin. After ten years absence, Solon returned to Athens, and found the city involved in slavery. Pisistratus had procured himself a guard formed of his own creatures, who at length seized on the citidel, while none were left, who had sufficient courage or conduct to oppose him.

In this general consternation, which was the result of folly on the one hand, and treachery on the other, the whole city was one scene of tumult and disorder, some flying, others inwardly complaining, others preparing for slavery with patient submission. Solon was the only man, who, without fear or shrinking, deplored the folly of the times, and reproached the Athenians with their cowardice and treachery. "You might with ease (said he) have crushed the tyrant in his bud; but nothing now remains but to pluck him up by the roots. As for myself, I have at least the satisfaction of having discharged my duty to my country and the laws: as for the rest, I have nothing to fear; and now, upon the destruction of my country, my only confidence is in my great age, which gives me the hopes of not being a long survivor." In fact, he did not survive the liberty of his country above two years; he died at Cyprus, in the eightieth year of his age, lamented and admired by every state of Greece. Besides his skill in legislation, Solon was remarakble for several other shining qualities: he was master of eloquence in so high a degree, that from him Cicero dates the origin of oratory in Athens. He was also successful in poetry; and Plato asserts, that it was only for want of due application, that he did not come to dispute the prize with Homer himself.

CHAP. III.

FROM the death of Solon, to about the year of the world 3500, Athens continued to be the scene of party cabals, and usurped tyranny; but, about this period, two young citizens began to diftinguifh themfelves at Athens, namely Ariftides and Themiftocles. Thefe youths were of very different difpofitions; but from this difference refulted the greateft advantages to their country. Themiftocles was naturally inclined to a popular government, and omitted nothing that could render him agreeable to the public, or gain him friends. His complaifance was boundlefs, and his defire to oblige fometimes outftepped the bounds of duty. His partiality was often confpicuous. Ariftides was remarkable for his juftice and integrity. Being a favourer of ariftocracy, in imitation of Lycurgus, he was friendly, but never at the expence of juftice. In feeking honours, he ever declined the interefts of his friends, left they fhould, in turn, demand his intereft when his duty was to be impartial. The love of the public good was the great fpring of all his actions, and with that in view no difficulties could daunt, no fuccefs or elevation exalt him. On all occafions he preferved his ufual calmnefs of temper, being perfuaded, that he was entirely his country's, and very little his own.

At this time, Darius, king of Perfia, was turning his arms againft Greece, while thefe illuftrious Athenians were infpiring their fellow citizens with a noble confidence in their bravery, and made every preparation for the expected invafion, which prudence and deliberate valour could fuggeft.

In the mean time, Darius' generals made themselves masters of the islands in the Ægean sea, and laid siege to Eretria, which they at last took by storm, owing to the treachery of some of the principal inhabitants. The town was plundered and burnt, and the inhabitants put in chains, and sent as the first fruits of war to the Persian monarch; but he, contrary to their expectations, treated them with great lenity, and gave them a village in the country of Cissa to live in.

This was soon followed by the battle of Marathon, the first great battle the Greeks had ever engaged in. It was not like any of their former contests arising from jealousy, and terminating in an easy accommodation: it was a battle that was to be decided with the greatest monarch of the earth. This was an engagement that was to decide the liberty of Greece, and, what was of infinitely greater moment, the future progress of refinement among mankind. Upon the event of this battle depended the complexion, which the manners of the West were hereafter to assume, whether they were to adopt Asiatic customs with their conquerors, or to go on in modelling themselves upon Grecian refinements. This therefore may be considered as one of the most important battles that ever was fought, and the event was as little to be expected as the success was glorious.

Miltiades, who was now invested with the supreme command of the Greek army, like an experienced general, endeavoured, by the advantage

vantage of his ground, to make up for his deficiency in strength and number, his whole army consisting but of ten thousand. He was sensible, that by extending his front to oppose the enemy, he must weaken it too much, and give their dense body the advantage. He therefore drew up his army at the foot of a mountain, so that the enemy should not surround him, or charge him in the rear. On the flanks, on either side, he caused large trees to be thrown, which were cut down for that purpose, and these served to guard him from the Persian cavalry, that generally wheeled on the flank in the heat of an engagement. Datis, the Persian general, was sensible of this advantageous disposition; but relying on his superiority of numbers, and unwilling to wait till Miltiades should receive reinforcements, he determined to engage.

The signal was no sooner given than the Athenians, without waiting the Persian onset, rushed in upon their ranks with desperate rapidity, as if wholly regardless of safety. The Persians considered this first step of the Athenians as the result of madness, and were more inclined to despise them as maniacs, than oppose them as soldiers. However, they were quickly undeceived. It had never been the custom of the Greeks to run on with this headlong valour; but comparing the number of their own forces with that of the enemy and expecting safety only from rashness, they determined to break through the enemy's ranks, or fall in the attempt. The greatness of their danger added to their courage, and despair did the rest. The Persians, however, stood their ground with great intrepidity, and the battle was long, fierce, and obstinate. Miltiades had made the wings of his army exceedingly strong, but had left the main body weaker, and not so deep; for having but ten thousand men to oppose such a numerous army, he supposed the victory could be obtained by no other means than by strengthening his flanks. He doubted not but that, when his wings were once victorious, they would be able to wheel upon the enemy's main body on either side, and then easily rout them. The Persians, therefore, finding the main body weakest, attacked it with their utmost vigour. It was in vain that Aristides and Themistocles, who were stationed in this post of danger, endeavoured to keep their troops to the charge: courage and intrepidity were unable to resist the torrent of encreasing numbers, so that they were at last obliged to give ground. In the mean time the wings were victorious; and now, just as the main body was fainting under the unequal encounter, these came up, and gave them time to recover their strength and order. Thus the scale of victory quickly turned in their favour, the Persians began to give ground in turn, and, being unsupported by fresh forces, they fled to their ships with the utmost precipitation. The confusion and disorder was now universal, the Athenians followed them to the beach, and set many of their ships on fire.

The Flight of the Persians at Marathon

On this occasion it was that Cyndœyrus, the brother of the poet Æschylus, seized with his hand one of the ships that the enemy was pushing off from the shore. The Persians within, seeing themselves thus stopped, cut off his right hand that held the prow; he then laid hold of it with his left, which they also cut off; at last, he seized it with his teeth, and in that manner expired.

Seven of the enemy's ships were taken, above six thousand Persians were slain, without reckoning those who were drowned in the sea as they endeavored to escape, or those who were consumed when the ships were set on fire. Of the Greeks, not above two hundred men were killed, among whom was Callimachus, who gave his vote for bringing on the engagement. The Persian forces, before the battle, consisted of six hundred ships, and an army of an hundred and twenty thousand men. Their instructions were, to give up Athens to be plundered, to burn all the houses and temples and to lead away all the inhabitants into slavery. The country was to be laid desolate, and the army was provided with chains and fetters for binding the conquered nations.

Thus ended the famous battle of Marathon, which the Persians were so sure of gaining, that they had brought marble into the field, in order to erect a trophy there. This battle was fought in the year of the world 3514.

A part of the army, immediately after the battle, marched forward to Athens, to protect it from any attempts the enemy might make,

which

which proved a very prudent measure; for the Persian fleet, instead of sailing directly back to Asia, made an attempt to surprise Athens, before they supposed the Greek troops could arrive from Marathon. The Athenian troops, however, took the precaution to move directly thither, and performed their march with so much expedition, that, though it was forty miles from Marathon, they arrived there in one day. In this manner the Greeks not only expelled their enemies, but confirmed their security. By this victory, the Grecians were taught to know their own strength, and not to tremble before an enemy only terrible in name.

The gratitude of the Athenians to Miltiades spoke a nobleness of mind, that far surpassed expensive triumphs, or base adulation. Sensible that his merits were too great for money to repay, they caused a picture to be painted by Polygnotus, one of their most celebrated artists, in which Miltiades was represented, at the head of the ten commanders, exhorting the soldiers, and setting them an example of their duty. This picture was preserved for many ages, with other paintings of the best masters, in the portico where Zeno afterwards instituted his school of philosophy. Every officer, as well as private soldier, who fell in this battle, had a monument erected to his memory on the plains of Marathon.

Though the gratitude of the Athenians to Miltiades was very sincere, yet it was of no long continuance. This fickle and jealous people, naturally capricious, and now more than ever

ever careful of preserving their freedom, were willing to take every opportunity of mortifying a general, from whose merit they had much to fear. Being appointed, with seventy ships, to punish those islands that had favoured the Persian invasion, he sailed to Paros, and invested that place. Here, having broken his thigh by an accident, he was obliged to raise the siege, and return home. On his arrival at Athens, the whole city began to murmur, and he was accused of having taken a bribe from Persia. As he was not in a condition to answer this charge, being confined to his bed by the wound he received at Paros, the accusation took place against him, and he was condemned to lose his life. However, in consideration of his former services, his sentence was commuted into a penalty of fifty talents, the sum which it had cost the state in fitting out the late unsuccessful expedition. Not being rich enough to pay this sum, he was thrown into prison, where his wound growing worse, from bad air and confinement, it turned at last to a gangrene, and put an end to his life and misfortunes. Thus perished a man, who has been very justly praised for his condescension, moderation, and justice. To him Athens was indebted for all its glory, he being the man who first taught her to despise the empty menaces of the boastful Persians. Cimon, his son, who was at this time very young, signalized his piety on this occasion. As this ungrateful city would not permit the body of Miltiades to be buried until all his debts were paid, this young man employed all

his

his interest among his friends, strained his utmost credit to pay the fine, and procured his father an honourable interment.

CHAP. IV.

DARIUS, king of Persia, died amidst the preparations he was making for a second expedition into Greece; but he was succeeded by a son, who inherited all his ambition, without any share of his abilities. He was a young man, surrounded by flatterers, and naturally vain and superficial. Having drained all the East to compose his own army, and the West to supply those of the Carthagenians, who were come to his aid, he set out from Susa, in order to enter on this war, ten years after the battle of Marathon, and in the year of the world 3523.

Sardis was the place, where the various nations that were compelled to his banner were to assemble. His fleet was to advance along the coast of Asia Minor towards the Hellespont; but as, in doubling the cape of Mount Athos, many ships were detained, he was resolved to cut a passage through that neck of land, which joined the mount to the continent, and thus gave his shipping a shorter and safer passage. This canal was a mile and a half long, and hollowed out from a high mountain. It required immense labour to perform so great a work; but his numbers and his ambition were sufficient to surmount all difficulties. To urge on the

the undertaking the faster, he treated his laborers with the greatest severity ; while, with all the ostentation of an eastern prince, he gave his commands to the mountains to sink before him : "Athos, (said he) thou proud aspiring mountain, that liftest up thy head unto the heavens, be not so audacious as to put obstacles in my way. If thou givest them that opposition, I will cut thee level to the plain, and throw thee headlong into the sea!"

Early in the spring, he directed his march down towards the Hellespont, where his fleet lay in all their pomp, expecting his arrival. Here he was desirous of taking a survey of all his forces, which composed an army that was never equalled either before or since. It was composed of the most powerful nations of the East, and of people scarce known to posterity, except by name. The remotest India contributed its supplies, while the coldest tracts of Scythia sent their assistance. Medes, Persians, Bactirans, Lydians, Assyrians, Hyrcanians, and an hundred other countries of various complexions, languages, dresses, and arms. The land army, which he brought out of Asia, consisted of seventeen hundred thousand foot, and fourscore thousand horse. Three hundred thousand more that were added upon crossing the Hellespont, made all his land forces together amount to above two millions of men. His fleet, when it set out from Asia, consisted of twelve hundred and seven vessels, each carrying two hundred men. The Europeans augmented his fleet with an hundred and twenty vessels, each of which carried two hundred men. Besides these, there were a thousand smaller vessels, fitted for carrying provisions and stores. The men contained in these, with the former, amounded to six hundred thousand: so that the whole army might be said to amount to two millions and a half, which, with the women, slaves, and settlers, always accompanying a Persian army, might make the whole above five millions of souls. Such was the state of this proud monarch's forces.

Lord of so many and such various subjects, Xerxes found a pleasure in reviewing his forces: beholding all the earth covered with his troops, and all the sea crouded with his vessels, he felt a secret joy diffuse itself through his frame, from the consciousness of his own superior power. But all the workings of this monarch's mind were in extreme: a sudden sadness soon took place of his pleasure, and dissolving into a shower of tears, he gave himself up to the reflection, that not one of so many thousands would be alive an hundred years after.

In the mean time Xerxes had given orders for building a bridge of boats across the Hellespont, for the transporting of his army into Europe. This narrow strait, which now goes by the name of the Dardanelles, is near an English mile over. However, soon after the completion of this work, a violent storm arising, the whole was broken and destroyed, and the labour was to be undertaken anew. The fury of Xerxes, upon this disappointment, was attended with equal extravagance and cruelty.

His

His vengeance knew no bounds, the workmen who had undertaken the task, had their heads struck off by his order; and that the sea also might know its duty, he ordered it to be lashed as a delinquent, and a pair of fetters to be thrown into it, to curb its future irregularities. Having thus given vent to his absurd resentment, two bridges were ordered to be built in the place of the former, one for the army to pass over, and the other for the baggage and beasts of burden. The workmen, now warned by the fate of their predecessors, undertook to give their labours greater stability: they placed three hundred and sixty vessels across the strait, some of them having three banks of oars, and others fifty oars a-piece. They then cast large anchors on both sides into the water, in order to fix those vessels against the violence of the winds and current. They then drove large piles into the earth, with huge rings fastened to them, to which were tied six vast cables, which went over each of the two bridges.— Over all these they laid trunks of trees, cut purposely for that use, and flat boats over them, fastened and joined together, so as to serve for a floor, or solid bottom. When the whole work was thus completed, a day was appointed for their passing over; and as soon as the first rays of the sun began to appear, sweet odours of all kinds were abundantly scattered over the new work, and the way was strewed with myrtle. At the same time, Xerxes, turning his face towards the east, worshipped the sun, which is the god of the Per-

fians. Then, throwing his libations into the
fea, together with a golden cup and Perſian
ſcymitar, he went forwards, and gave orders
for the army to follow. This immenſe train
were no leſs than ſeven days and ſeven nights
paſſing over, while thoſe who were appointed
to conduct the march, quickened the troops by
laſhing them along; for the ſoldiers of the Eaſt,
at that time, and to this day, are treated like
ſlaves. Thus this immenſe army having landed
in Europe, and being joined by the ſeveral European nations that acknowledged the Perſian
power, Xerxes prepared for marching directly
forward into Greece.

He continued his march through Thrace,
Macedonia, and Theſſaly, every knee bending
before him till he came to the ſtraits of Thermopylæ, where he firſt found an enemy prepared
to diſpute his paſſage. This army was a body
of Spartans, led on by Leonidas their king,
who had been ſent thither to oppoſe him.
None of the Grecian ſtates were found bold
enough to face this formidable army but Athens
and Lacedæmon. One cannot, without aſtoniſhment, reflect on the intrepidity of theſe two
ſtates, who determined to face the innumerable
army of Xerxes with ſuch diſproportioned forces.
Their whole army amounted to only eleven
thouſand two hundred men. Ariſtides was
called from baniſhment, and placed at the head
of their forces.

It was ſoon reſolved to ſend a body of men
to guard the paſs at Thirmopylæ, where a few
would be capable of acting againſt numbers.
Thirmopylæ was a narrow paſs of twenty-five

feet broad, between Theſſaly and Phocis, defended by the remains of a wall, with gates to it. This place was pitched upon, as well for the narrowneſs of the way, as for its vicinity to the ſea, from whence the land forces could occaſionally receive aſſiſtance from the fleet. The command of this important paſs was given to Leonidas, one of the kings of Sparta, who led thither a body of ſix thouſand men. They were all along taught to look upon themſelves as a forlorn hope, only placed there to check the progreſs of the enemy, and give them a foretaſte of the deſperate valour of Greece. Even oracles were not wanting to check their ardour; for it had been declared, that to procure the ſafety of Greece it was neceſſary that a king, one of the deſcendants of Hercules, ſhould die. This taſk was cheerfully undertaken by Leonidas; and as he marched out from Lacedæmon, he conſidered himſelf as a willing victim offered up for the good of his country. However, he joyfully put himſelf at the head of his little band, took poſſeſſion of his poſt, and with deliberate deſperation waited at Thirmopylæ for the coming up of the Perſian army.

In the mean time, Xerxes approached with his numerous army, fluſhed with ſucceſs, and confident of victory. His camp exhibited all the marks of Eaſtern magnificence and Aſiatic luxury. As he expected to meet no obſtructions on his way to Greece, he was ſurpriſed to find, that a handful of men would dare to diſpute his paſſage. He waited four days to give the Greeks time to retire; but they continued their poſt,

post amusing themselves in their usual way.— He sent to them to deliver up their arms; but Leonidas, with a truly Spartan spirit, desired him *to come and take them*. Xerxes offered, if they would lay down their arms, to recieve them as friends, and to give them a country much lager and better than what they fought for. "No country (they replied) was worth acceptance, unless won by virtue; and as for their arms, they should want them, whether as his friends or enemies."

Xerxes, thus treated with contempt, at length ordered a body of Medes to advance, who began the onset, but were repulsed with great loss. The number of the assailants only served to increase their confusion; and it now began to appear, that Xerxes had many followers, but few soldiers. These forces being routed by the Grecian troops, the Persian immortal band was brought up; but these were as unsuccessful as the former. Thus did the Greeks keep their ground for two days, and no power on earth seemed capable of removing them from their advantageous situation. The Persians, however, by the treachery of a Grecian deserter, got possession of an advantageous post, which commanded the rear of the Spartans.

Leonidas, apprized of this misfortune, and seeing that his post was no longer tenable, advised the troops of his allies to retire, and reserve themselves for better times, and the future safety of Greece. As for himself, and his fellow Spartans, they were obliged by their laws not to fly; that he owed a life to his country;

and

and that it was now his duty to fall in its defence. Having thus dismissed all but his three hundred Spartans, with some Thespians and Thebans, in all not a thousand men, he exhorted his followers, in the most cheerful manner, to prepare for death. "Come, my fellow-soldiers, said he, let us dine cheerfully here, for to-night we shall sup with Pluto." His men, upon hearing his determined purpose, set up a loud shout, as if they had been invited to a banquet, and resolved every man to sell his life as dearly as he could. The night now began to advance, and this was thought the most glorious opportunity of meeting death in the enemy's camp. Thus resolved, they made directly to the Persian tents, and, in the darkness of the night, had almost reached the royal pavilion, with hopes of surprising the king. The obscurity added much to the horror of the scene; and the Persians, falling upon each other without distinction, rather assisted the Grecians than defended themselves. Thus success seemed to crown the rashness of their enterprize, until the morning beginning to dawn, the light discovered the smallness of their numbers. They were then soon surrounded by the Persian forces, who fearing to fall in upon them, flung their javelins from every quarter, till the Greeks, not so much conquered as tired with conquering, fell amidst heaps of the slaughtered enemy, leaving behind them an example of intrepidity never known before. Leonidas was one of the first that fell, and the endeavours of the Lacedæmonians to defend his dead body were incredible. Of all the train, two only escaped, who were treated with contempt and infamy.

The loss of Xerxes in this battle was said to amount to twenty thousand men, among whom were two of his brothers. Xerxes, therefore, dismayed at an obstinacy that cost him so dear, was for some time more inclined to try his fortune at sea, than to proceed immediately into the country, where he was informed, eight thousand Spartans, such as he had but lately fought with, were ready to receive him. Accordingly, the very day of the battle of Thirmopylæ, there was an engagement at sea between the two fleets. The Grecian fleet consisted of two hundred and seventy-one vessels: that of the enemy had lately lost four hundred vessels in a shipwreck, but were still greatly superior to the Grecian fleet.

Xerxes, to repair his loss by a victory, ordered two hundred Persian vessels to take a compass, and surprise the Grecians lying in the straits of Eubæa; but the Grecians, being apprised of their designs, set sail by night, and so, by a counter-surprise, fell in with them while they were thus separated from the main body, took and sunk thirty, forced the rest to sea, and there, by stress of weather, they were all soon after sunk or stranded. Enraged at these disappointments, the Persians bore down the next day with the whole fleet, and drawing up in form of an half-moon, made an offer of battle, which the Greeks as readily accepted. The Athenians having been reinforced with three and fifty sail, the battle was very obstinate and
bloody,

bloody, and the success pretty nearly equal on both sides, so that both parties seemed content to retire in good order.

After this, Xerxes, having entered the country of Phocis with his numerous army, plundered and burned every town through which he passed. Having sent off a considerable detachment to plunder the temple at Delphos, with the rest he marched down into Attica, where he found Athens deserted by all but a few in the citadel. These men despairing of succour, and unwilling to survive the loss of their country, would listen to no terms of accommodation ; they boldly withstood the first assault, and, warmed by the enthusiasm of religion, began to hope for success. However, a second assault carried their feeble outworks, they were all put to the sword, and the citadel reduced to ashes.

In the mean time, the confederate Greeks determined in council, that they should prepare to receive the Persians on the isthmus by land, and in the straits of Salamis by sea. Xerxes, after having demolished and burned Athens, marched down towards the sea, to act in conjunction with his fleet, which he had determined should once more come to an engagement with the enemy. The Grecian fleet consisted of three hundred and eighty ships, the Persian fleet was much more numerous ; but whatever advantage they had in numbers, and the size of their ships, they fell infinitely short of the Greeks in their naval skill, and their acquaintance with the seas where they fought.

Themistocles, watching a favorable opportunity, gave the signal for battle, when the Grecian fleet sailed forward, in exact order. Xerxes, imputing his former ill success at sea to his own absence, was resolved to be a witness of the present engagement from the top of a promontory, where he caused a throne to be erected for that purpose. The Persians, therefore, advanced with such courage and impetuosity, as struck the enemy with terror; but their ardor abated when the engagement became closer. The numerous disadvantages of their circumstances then began to appear: the wind blew directly in their faces; the height and heaviness of their vessels made them unwieldy and useless; even the number of their ships, in the narrow seas where they fought, only served to embarrass and encrease their confusion. The Ionians first gave way, then the Phœnicians, and Cyprians, when the rest retired in great disorder, and fell foul of each other in their retreat. The Greeks pursued the Persian fleet on every side; some were intercepted at the straits of Attica, many were sunk, and more taken. Above two hundred were burnt, all the rest were dispersed; and the allies, dreading the resentment of the Greeks, as well as of the Persian king, made the best of their way to their own country. Such was the success of the battle of Salamis, in which the Persians received a severer blow than they had ever before experienced from Greece.

Xerxes being heartily tired of this disgraceful business, left his generals to take care of his army,

army, and hastened with a small retinue to the sea-side, which he reached forty-five days after the battle of Salamais. When he arrived at that place, he found the bridge broken down by the violence of the waves, in a tempest that had lately happened. He was, therefore, obliged to pass the strait in a small boat; which manner of returning, being compared with the ostentatious method in which he had set out, rendered his disgrace still more poignant and afflicting. The army, which he had ordered to follow him, having been unprovided with provisions, suffered great hardships by the way. After having consumed all the corn they could find, they were obliged to live upon herbs, and even upon the bark and leaves of trees. Thus harrassed and fatigued, a pestilence began to complete their misery; and, after a fatiguing journey of forty-five days, in which they were pursued rather by vultures and beasts of prey, than by men, they came to the Hellespont, where they crossed over, and marched from thence to Sardis. Such was the end of Xerxes's expedition into Greece: a measure begun in pride, and terminated in infamy and disgrace.

CHAP. V.

THE joy of the Greeks, on the victory of Salamais, was general and loud, and Themistocles was loaded with glory. Mardonius, whom Xerxes had left in Greece with a numerous

rous army; was soon after killed in battle, and all his forces completely routed. Thus ended the invasion of Greece, nor ever after was the Persian army seen to cross the Hellespont.—During these events, Xerxes lay at Sardis, expecting a reversion of his fortune; but messengers coming every hour, loaded with the news of some fatal disaster, and finding himself unable to retrieve his affairs, he retired further into the country, and endeavoured to drown in luxury and riot the uneasy reflections of his successless ambition. To the want of success abroad was added the contempt of his subjects at home; and this brought on a train of treasons, insurrections, sacrilege, murder, incest, and cruelty: so that the latter part of his reign was as scandalous, as the first part of it had been unfortunate.

The state of Athens, being thus in a great measure freed from its fears of a foreign enemy, began to cherish intestine animosities, and its citizens laboured with every art to supplant each other in aiming at places of trust and authority. But the conduct of Aristides, in the discharge of his duty on all occasions, confirmed the great opinion mankind had formed of his integrity.

Aristides presided over the treasury with the care of a father over his family, and the caution of a miser over what he holds dearer than his life. No man complained of his administration, and no part of the public money was exhausted in vain. He, who thus contributed to make government rich, was himself poor;
and

and so far was he from being ashamed of poverty, that he considered it as glorious to him as all the victories he had won. Aristides asserted, that he only might be said to want, who permitted his appetites to transgress the bounds of his income: and that he, who could dispense with a few things, thus rendered himself more like the gods who want nothing.

Thus he lived, just in his public, and independent in his private character. His house was a public school for virtue, and was open to all young Athenians who sought wisdom, or were ambitious of power. He gave them the kindest reception, heard them with patience, instructed them with familiarity, and endeavoured, above all things, to give them a just value for themselves. History does not mention the exact time or place of his death; but it pays the most glorious testimony to his disinterested character, in telling us, that he who had the absolute disposal of all the public treasures died poor. It is even asserted, that he did not leave money enough behind him to pay the expences of his funeral, but that the government was obliged to bear the charge of it, and to maintain his family. His daughters were married, and his son subsisted, at the expence of the public; and some of his grandchildren were supported by a pension, equal to that which such received, who had been victorious at the Olympic games. But the greatest honour that his countrymen paid to his memory, was in giving him the title of Just, a character far superior to all the empty titles of wisdom or conquest; since fortune or accident may confer wisdom or valour, but the virtues of morality are solely of our own making.

About the year of the world 3572, a rupture happened between the Athenians and the Lacedæmonians; and thus the Grecian states, having now no foreign enemy to disturb them, began to harrass and depopulate each other. But a more terrible punishment now began to threaten them from nature: a plague broke out in the city of Athens, a more terrible one than which is scarcely recorded in the annals of history. It is related, that it began in Ethiopia, from thence descended into Egypt, then travelled into Lybia and Persia, and at last broke out like a flood upon Athens. This pestilence baffled the utmost efforts of art; the most robust constitutions were unable to withstand its attacks; no skill could obviate, nor no remedy dispel the terrible infection. The instant a person was seized, he was struck with despair, which quite disabled him from attempting a cure. The humanity of friends was as fatal to themselves, as it was ineffectual to the unhappy sufferers. Most of the inhabitants, for want of lodging, lived in little cottages, in which they could scarce breathe, while the burning heat of the summer encreased the pestilential malignity. They were seen confusedly huddled together, the dead as well as the dying; some crawling through the streets, some lying along by the sides of fountains, whither they had endeavored to repair, to quench the raging thirst that consumed them. Their very temples were filled with dead bodies, and every

part

part of the city exhibited a dreadful scene of mortality, without the least remedy for the present, or the least hopes with regard to futurity. It seized the people with such violence, that they fell one upon another as they passed along the streets. It was also attended with such uncommon pestilential vapours, that the very beasts and birds of prey, though famishing round the walls of the city, would not touch the bodies of those who died of it. Even in those who recovered, it left such a tincture of its malignity, that it struck upon their senses. It effaced the memory of all the passages of their former lives, and they knew neither themselves, nor their nearest relations. Such was the effects of this dreadful pestilence; but of the manner in which it ended, and of the numbers destroyed by it, we have no certain account.

We shall pass over many particulars of the Peloponnesian war, as they afford only a wretched scene of the citizens of one Grecian state staining their hands with the blood of others; but we shall be more particular in mentioning the actions and character of those heroes and philosophers, who flourished during that period. Among these, Pericles formed no inconsiderable character. He was descended from the greatest and most illustrious families of Athens; his father, Xanthippus, defeated the Persians at Mycale, and his mother, Agarista, was niece to Calisthenes, who expelled the tyrants, and established a popular government in Athens. He had early thoughts of

rising

rising in the state, and took lessons from Anaxagoras, in the philosophy of nature. He studied politics with great assiduity, but particularly devoted himself to eloquence, which, in a popular state, he considered as the fountain of all promotion. His studies were crowned with success; and the poets, his contemporaries, affirm, that his eloquence was so powerful, that, like thunder, he shook and astonished all Greece. He had the art of uniting force and beauty; there was no resisting the strength of his arguments, or the sweetness of his delivery. Thucydides, his great opponent, was often heard to say, that though he had often overthrown him, the power of his persuasion was such, that the audience could never perceive him fallen.

To this eloquence he added also a thorough insight into human nature, as well as a perfect acquaintance with the disposition of his auditors. It was a constant saying with him to himself, "Remember, Pericles, thou art going to speak to men born in the arms of Liberty, and do thou take care to flatter them in their ruling passion." He resembled the tyrant Pisistratus, not only in the sweetness of his voice, but the features of his face, and his whole air and manner. To these natural and acquired graces, he added those of fortune: he was very rich, and had an extensive alliance with all the most powerful families of the state.

The death of Aristides, and some other favourable circumstances, gave opportunities to
his

his growing ambition: yet he at first concealed his designs with the most cautious reserve, till finding the people encrease in his interest, he set himself at their head, and opposed the principal men of the state with great appearance of disinterested virtue. The chief obstacle to his rise was Cimon, whose candour and liberality had gained him a numerous party of all ranks and denominations. In opposition to him, Pericles called in popular assistance, and by expending the public money in bribes, largesses, and other distributions, he easily gained the multitude to espouse his interests.

Having thus laid a secure foundation in popularity, he next struck at the council of the Areopagus, which was composed of the most respectable persons of all Athens; and, by the assistance of one Ephialtes, another popular champion, he drew away most causes from the cognizance of that court, and brought the whole order into contempt. In this manner, while Cimon was permitted to conduct the war abroad, he managed all the supplies at home; and, as it was his interest to keep Cimon at a distance, he took care to provide him with a sufficiency of foreign employment.

Pericles every day gained new ground, till he at last found himself possessed of the authority of the whole state. It was then that he began to change his behaviour, and from acting the humble and fawning suppliant, he assumed the haughty airs of royalty. He now no longer submitted himself to the caprice of the people, but changed the democratic state of Athens in-

to

to a kind of monarchy, without departing, however, from the public good. He would sometimes, indeed, win his fellow-citizens over to his will; but at other times, when he found them obstinate, he would in a manner compel them to consult their own interests.—Thus between power and pursuasion, public profusion, and private œconomy, political falsehoods, and private integrity, Pericles became the principal ruler at Athens, and all such as were his enemies became the enemies of the state.

Fickleness and inconstancy, however, were the prevailing characters of the Athenians; and, as these carried them on to their greatest excesses, they soon brought them back within the bounds of moderation and prudence. Pericles had long been a favourite, but the state having suffered great calamities, he at last came to be obnoxious: they had deposed him from the command of the army; but soon repented of their rashness, and reinstated him, a short time after, with more than former authority.—However, he did not live long to enjoy his honours. He was seized with the plague, which, like a malignant enemy, struck its severest blow at parting. Being extremely ill, and ready to breathe his last, the principal citizens, and such of his friends that had not forsaken him, discoursing concerning the loss they were about to sustain, ran over his exploits, and computed the number of his victories. They did not imagine that Pericles attended to what they said, as he seemed insen-
sible;

sible; but it was far otherwise, as not a single word of their discourse had escaped him. At last, cried he, " Why will you extol a series of actions, in which Fortune had the greatest part? There is one circumstance which I would not have forgotten, yet which you have passed over: I could wish to have it remembered, as the most glorious circumstance of my life, that I never yet caused a single citizen to put on mourning." Thus died Pericles, in whom were united a number of excellent qualities without impairing each other. He was as well skilled in naval affairs as in the conduct of armies; as well skilled in the arts of raising money as of employing it; eloquent in public, and pleasing in private; he was a patron of artists, at once informing them by his taste and example.

Not long after the death of Pericles, the Athenians and Lacedæmonians made peace, and every thing now promised a restoration of former tranquility; but a new promoter of troubles was now beginning to make his appearance, and from him, those who wished for peace had every thing to fear: this was the celebrated Alcibiades, the disciple of Socrates, a youth equally remarkable for the beauty of his person, and the graces of his mental accomplishments.

The strict intimacy between Alcibiades and Socrates is one of the most remarkable circumstances of his life. This philosopher observing excellent natural qualities in him, which were greatly heightened by the beauty of his person,

bestowed

bestowed incredible pains in cultivating so valuable a plant, lest, being neglected, it should wither as it grew, and in the end degenerate. Alcibiades, indeed, was exposed to numberless dangers: the greatness of his extraction, his vast riches, the authority of his family, the credit of his guardians, his personal talents, and, still more than these, the flattery and complaisance of all who approached him.

Notwithstanding the strong endeavours that were used to divert this young Athenian from a correspondence, which alone was capable of securing him from so many snares, he devoted himself entirely to it. He had the most unbounded wit; he was fully sensible of Socrates' extraordinary merit, and could not resist the charms of his sweetly insinuating eloquence, which at that time, had a greater ascendant over him than the alurements of pleasure. He was so zealous a disciple of that great master, that he followed him wherever he went, took the utmost delight in his conversation, received his instructions, and even his reprimands, with wonderful docility, and was so moved with his discourses, as even to shed tears, and abhor himself: so weighty was the force of truth in the mouth of Socrates, and in so odious a light did he shew the vices, to which Alcibiades began to abandon himself.

Alcibiades, in those moments when he listened to Socrates, differed so much from himself, that he appeared quite another man. However, his head-strong fiery temper, and his natural fondness for pleasure, which was heightened

ened and enflamed by the difcourfes and advifes of young people, foon plunged him into his former irregularities, and tore him as it were from his mafter, who was obliged to purfue him as a flave who had efcaped correction. This viciffitude of flights and returns of virtuous refolutions, and relapfes into vice, continued a long time; but ftill Socrates was not difgufted with his levity, and always flattered himfelf with the hopes of bringing him back to his duty. Hence certainly arofe the ftrong mixture of good and evil that always appeared in his conduct, the inftructions his mafter had given him fometimes prevailing, and, at other times, the fire of his paffion hurrying him, in a manner, againft his own will, into things of a quite oppofite nature. Among the various paffions that were difcovered in him, the ftrongeft and moft prevailing was a haughty turn of mind, which would force all things to fubmit to it, and could not bear a fuperior, or even an equal.

Alcibiades, with fuch a caft of mind as we have defcribed, was not born for repofe, and had fet every engine at work to reverfe the treaty lately concluded between the Athenians and Lacedæmonians. He was difgufted with the latter, becaufe they directed themfelves only to Nicias, of whom they had a very high opinion; and, on the contrary, feemed to take no manner of notice of him, though his anceftors had enjoyed the rights of hofpitality among them.

Having found means to carry his point against the Lacedæmonians, he was declared general, and appointed to command the fleet; but was soon afterwards disgraced. After having experienced strange vicissitudes of fortune, being sometimes banished or condemned to death by the Athenians, at other times at the head of their fleets and armies, he at last took shelter at the court of Persia, where the Lacedæmonians found means to persuade that monarch to dispatch him. Alcibiades was then in a small town in Phrigia, where he lived with his concubine Timandra. Those who were sent to kill him, not daring to enter his house, contented themselves with surrounding and letting it on fire. Alcibiades having quitted it through the flames, sword in hand, the barbarians were afraid to stay to come to blows with him, but flying and retreating as he advanced, they poured their darts and arrows upon him from a distance, and he fell dead upon the spot. Timandra took up his body, and having adorned and covered it with the finest robes she had, she made as magnificent a funeral for it as her condition would admit.

Such was the end of Alcibiades, whose great virtues were stifled and suppressed by still greater vices. It is not easy to say, whether his good or bad qualities were most pernicious to his country; for with the one he deceived, and with the other he oppressed it. In him distinguished valour was united with nobility of blood. He was eloquent, of great ability in affairs, insinuating, and formed for charming

all

all mankind. He loved glory, but indulged at the same time, his inclination for pleasure; nor was he so fond of pleasure, as to neglect his glory for it. He knew how to give into, or abstract himself from, the allurements of luxury, according to the situation of his affairs. Never was there ductility of genius equal to his: he metamorphosed himself, with incredible facility, into the most contrary forms, and supported them all with as much ease and grace as if each had been natural to him.

The death of Alcibiades naturally leads us to give the character of his master, one of the greatest philosophers that the world perhaps ever produced, the immortal Socrates. He was the son of an obscure citizen of Athens, and, emerging from the meanness of his birth, he gave astonishing examples of courage, moderation and wisdom. He opposed the power of the thirty tyrants, who had usurped the government of Athens, and spoke loudly against the bigotry and prosecution of the times. He possessed unexampled good nature, and an universal love to mankind. As it was very difficult to correct the aged, and to make people change principles, who revere the errors in which they are grown grey, he devoted his labours principally to the instruction of youth, in order to sow the seeds of virtue in a soil more fit to produce the fruits of it. He had no open school like the rest of the philosophers, nor set times for his lessons. He had no benches prepared, nor even mounted a professor's chair; he was the philosopher of all times

times and seasons; he taught in all places, and upon all occasions; in walking, conversation at meals, in the army, and in the midst of the camp, in the public assembly of the senate or people. Such was the man, whom a faction in the city had long devoted to destruction: he had been, for many years before his death, the object of their satire and ridicule.

Aristophanes, the comic poet, was engaged to expose him on the stage: he composed a piece called The Clouds, wherein he introduced the philosopher in a basket, uttering the most ridiculous absurdities. This was the first blow struck at him; but it was not till twenty years afterwards that Melites appeared in a more formal manner as his accuser, and entered a regular process against him. His accusation consisted of two heads: the first was, that he did not admit the gods acknowledged by the republic, and introduced new divinities; the second, that he corrupted the youth of Athens; and concluded with inferring, that sentence of death ought to be passed against him. How far the whole charge affected him is not easy to determine: It is certain, that amid so much zeal and superstition as then reigned in Athens, he never dared openly to oppose the received religion, and was therefore forced to preserve an outward shew of it; but it is very probable, from the discourses he frequently held with his friends, that in his heart he despised and laughed at their monstrous opinions and ridiculous mysteries, as having no other foundation than the fables of the poets; and that he

had

had attained to the notion of the one only true God, infomuch that, upon the account both of his belief of the Deity, and the exemplarinels of his life, fome have thought fit to rank him among the Chriftian philofophers.

Upon the day affigned, the proceedings commenced in the ufual forms, the parties appeared before the judges, and Melitus fpoke. The worfe his caufe, and the lefs it was provided with proofs, the more occafion he had for addrefs and art to cover its weaknefs. He omitted nothing that might render Socrates odious; and inftead of reafons, which could not but fail him, he fubftituted the delufive glitter of a lively and pompous eloquence. Socrates' defence is confidered as fo great a mafterpiece of ancient oratory, that even the narrow limits this work is confined to, will not permit of our paffing it over in filence.

"I am accufed (faid Socrates) of corrupting the youth, and of inftilling dangerous maxims into them, as well in regard to the worfhip of the gods, as the rules of government. You know, Athenians, that I never made it my profeffion to teach, nor can envy, however violent againft me, reproach me with having fold my inftructions. I have an undeniable evidence for me in this refpect, which is my poverty. I was always equally ready to communicate my thoughts either to the rich or poor, and to give them entire leifure to queftion or anfwer me. My whole employment is to perfuade the young and old againft too much love for the body, for riches, all other

precarious

precarious things, of whatsoever nature they be; and against too little regard for the soul, which ought to be the object of their affection: for I incessantly urge upon you, that virtue does not proceed from riches, but, on the contrary, riches from virtue; and that all the other goods of human life, as well public as private, have their source in the same principle.

"If to speak in this manner be to corrupt youth, I confess, Athenians, that I am guilty, and deserve to be punished. If what I say be not true, it is most easy to convict me of my falsehoods. I see here a great number of my disciples: they have only to appear. But, perhaps, the reserve and consideration for a master who has instructed them, will prevent them from declaring against me; at least, their fathers, brothers, and uncles, cannot, as good relations and good citizens, dispense with their not standing forth to demand vengeance against the corrupter of their sons, brothers, and nephews. But these are the persons who take upon them my defence, and interest themselves in the success of my cause.

"Pass on me what sentence you please, Athenians; but I can neither repent nor change my conduct: I must not abandon or suspend a function, which God himself has imposed on me. If, after having faithfully kept all the posts wherein I was placed by our general at Potidæa, Amphipolis, and Delium, the fear of death should at this time make me abandon that, in which the divine Providence has

placed

placed me, by commanding me to pass my life in the study of philosophy, for the instruction of myself and others; this would be a most criminal desertion indeed, and make me highly worthy of being cited before this tribunal as an impious man, who does not believe the gods. Should you resolve to acquit me, for the future, I should not hesitate to make answer, Athenians, I honor and love you, but I shall choose rather to obey God than you, and to my latest breath shall never renounce my philosophy, nor cease to exhort and reprove you, according to my custom, by telling each of you, when you come in my way, My good friend and citizen of the most famous city in the world for wisdom and valour, are you not ashamed to have no other thoughts than that of amassing wealth, and of acquiring glory, credit, and dignities, whilst you neglect the treasures of prudence, truth, and wisdom, and take no pains in rendering your soul as good and perfect as it is capable of being.

"I am reproached with abject fear and meanness of spirit, for being so busy in imparting my advice to every one in private and for having avoided to be present in your assemblies, to give my counsel to my country. I think I have sufficiently proved my courage and fortitude, both in the field, where I have borne arms with you, and in the senate when I opposed the violence and cruel orders of the thirty tyrants.

"For the rest, Athenians, if, in the extreme danger I now am, I do not imitate the behaviour of those, who, upon less emergencies, have implored and supplicated their judges with tears, and have brought forth their children, relations, and friends, it is not through pride and obstinancy, or any contempt for you, but solely for your honor, and for that of the whole city. You should know, that there are among our citizens those, who do not regard death as an evil, and who give that name only to injustice and infamy. At my age, and with the reputation, true or false, which I have, would it be consistent for me, after all the lessons I have given upon the contempt of death, to be afraid of it myself, and to belie in my last actions all the principles and sentiments of my past life?

"But without speaking of my fame, which I should extremely injure by such a conduct, I do not think it allowable to intreat a judge, nor to be absolved by supplications. He ought to be persuaded and convinced. The judge does not sit upon the bench to shew favour, by violating the laws; but to do justice in conforming to them. He does not swear to discharge with impunity whom he pleases, but to do justice where it is due. We ought not, therefore, to accustom you to perjury, nor you to suffer yourselves to be accustomed to it; for, in so doing, both the one and the other of us equally injure justice and religion, and both are criminals.

"Do not, therefore, expect from me, Athenians, that I should have recourse among you to means, which I believe neither honest nor
lawful;

lawful; especially upon this occasion, wherein I am accused of impiety by Melitus; for, if I should influence you by my prayers, and thereby induce you to violate your oaths, it would be undeniably evident, that I teach you not to believe in the gods; and even in defending and justifying myself, I should furnish my adversaries with arms against me, and prove that I believe no divinity. But I am very far from such bad thoughts: I am more convinced of the existence of God than my accusers; and so convinced, that I abandon myself to God and you, that you may judge of me as you shall deem best for yourselves."

Socrates pronounced this discourse with a firm and intrepid tone: his air, his action, his visage, expressed nothing of the accused; he seemed the master of his judges, from the assurance and greatness of his soul with which he spoke, without however losing any thing of the modesty natural to him. But how slight soever the proofs were against him, the faction was powerful enough to find him guilty, and his death was certainly a concerted thing.

By his first sentence, the judges only declared Socrates guilty; but when, by his answer, he appeared to appeal from their tribunal to that of justice and posterity; when, instead of confessing himself guilty, he demanded rewards and honour from the state, the judges were so very much offended, that they condemned him to drink hemlock, a method of execution in use among them.

Socrates

Socrates received this sentence with the utmost composure. Apollodorus, one of his disciples launching out into bitter invectives, and lamenting that his master should die *innocent*, " What, (replied Socrates, with a smile,) would you have me die guilty ? Melytus and Ayntus may kill, but they cannot hurt me."

After his sentence, he still continued with the same serene and intrepid aspect, with which he had long enforced virtue, and held tyrants in awe. When he entered his prison, which now became the residence of virtue and probity, his friends followed him thither, and continued to visit him during the interval between his condemnation and death, which lasted for thirty days.

The day before the death of Socrates, Crito, his intimate friend, went to him early in the morning to let him know, that it depended only on himself to quit the prison ; that the jailor was gained ; that he would find the doors open, and offered him a safe retreat in Thessaly. Socrates laughed at his proposal, and answered, that he reverenced the laws of his country, and resolved to obey them in all things, even in his death.

Socrates employed the last day of his life in entertaining his friends on the great and important subject of death ; he explained to them all the arguments for believing the soul to be immortal, and refuted all the objections against it. After he came out of the bath, his children were brought to him, for he had three;

two very little, and the other grown up. He spoke to them for some time, gave orders to the women who took care of them, and then dismissed them. Being returned into his chamber, he laid himself down upon his bed.

The keeper of the prison entered at the same instant, and having informed him, that the time for drinking the hemlock was come, which was at sun set, the keeper was so much afflicted with sorrow, that he turned his back and fell a weeping. The fatal cup, however, was at last brought, and Socrates asked what it was necessary for him to do. "Nothing more (replied the officer) than as soon as you have drank off the draught, to walk about till you find your legs grow weary, and afterwards to lie down upon your bed." He took the cup without any emotion, or change in his colour or countenance, and regarding the man, with a steady and assured look, "Well, (said he) what say you of this drink: may one make a libation out of it?" Upon being told, there was only enough for one dose, "At least, (continued he) we may say our prayers to the gods, as it is our duty, and implore them to make our exit from this world, and our last stage happy, which is what I most earnestly beg of them." After having spoken these words, he kept silence for some time, and then drank off the whole draught with an amazing tranquility and serenity of aspect, not to be expressed or conceived.

Till then his friends, with great violence to themselves, had refrained from tears; but after he had drank the potion, they were no longer their own masters, and wept abundantly. Apollodorus, who had been in tears during almost the whole conversation, began then to raise great cries, and to lament with such excessive grief, as pierced the hearts of all that were present. Socrates alone remained unmoved, and even reproved his friends, though with his usual mildness and good nature. " What are you doing? (said he to them) Oh! what is become of your virtue! Was it not for this I sent away the women, that they might not fall into these weaknesses? I have always heard you say, that we ought to die peaceably, and blessing the gods. Be at ease, I beg you, and shew more constancy and resolution." He then obliged them to restrain their tears.

In the mean time he kept walking to and fro; and, when he found his legs grow weary, he laid down upon his bed, as he had been directed. The poison then operated more and more. When Socrates found it began to gain upon the heart, uncovering his face, which had been covered, without doubt, to prevent any thing from disturbing him in his last moments, " Crito, (said he) we owe a cock to Æsculapius: discharge that vow for me, and pray do not forget it." Soon after this, he breathed his last. Crito went to his body, and closed his mouth and eyes. Such was the end of Socrates, in the first year of the ninety-fifth olympiad, and in the seventieth of his age.

It

It was not till some time after the death of this great man, that the people of Athens perceived their mistake, and began to repent of it. Their hatred being satisfied, their prejudices expired, and time having given them an opportunity for reflection, the notorious injustice of the sentence appeared in all its horrors. Nothing was heard throughout the city but discourses in favour of Socrates. The Academy, the Lycæum, private houses, publick walks, and market-places, seemed still to re-echo the sound of his loved voice. " Here (said they) he formed our youth, and taught our children to love their country, and to honor their parents. In this place he gave us his admirable lessons, and sometimes made us seasonable reproaches, to engage us more warmly in the pursuit of virtue. Alas! how have we rewarded him for such important services!" Athens was in universal mourning and consternation. The schools were shut up, and all exercises suspended. His accusers were called to account for the innocent blood they had caused to be shed: Melitus was condemned to die, and the rest banished. Plutarch observes, that all those, who had any share in this black calumny, were held in such abomination among the citizens, that no one would give them fire, answer them any question, nor go into the same bath with them; and they had the place cleaned where they had bathed, lest they should be polluted by touching it, which drove them into such despair, that many of them killed themselves. The Athenians, not contented

with

with having punished his accusers, caused a statue of brass to be erected to him, of the workmanship of the celebrated Lysippus, who placed it in one of the most conspicuous parts of the city. Their respect and gratitude rose even to a religious veneration: they dedicated a chapel to him, as to a hero and demi-god, which they called the chapel of Socrates.

CHAP. VI.

THE Athenians had hitherto taken the lead in the Grecian states; but the Spartans, who had completely conquered them, became their masters, and sunk them into obscurity.

At this period, Agesilaus, who was chosen king of Sparta, was sent into Asia with an army, under pretence of freeing the Grecian cities. He gained a signal victory over the Persian general, Tissaphernes, near the river Pactolus, where he forced the enemy's camp, and found considerable plunder. This success induced the Persian monarch, instead of meeting Agesilaus openly in the field, to subvert his interest among the Grecian states by the power of bribery; and indeed this confederacy was now so weakened, its concord and unanimity so totally destroyed, that they were open to every offer. The love of money was now rooted in their affections, and the Spartans were the only people that, for a while, seemed to disdain it; but the contagion still spreading, even they at

last

last yielded to its allurements, and every man fought private emolument, without attending to the good of his country.

The Spartans, however, being freed from the terror of foreign enemies, proceeded to spread terror among the petty states of Greece, whom they compelled to pay obedience to their will. These proceedings of the Spartans, however, gave birth to a powerful confederacy against them; and, through a succession of engagements, both by sea and land, the Spartans grew every day weaker, and their enemies more daring.

It soon began to appear, that the Thebans, one of the states of Greece, lately oppressed by the Spartans, were growing into power; and, while Sparta and Athens were weakening each other by mutual contests, this state, which had enjoyed all the emoluments, without any of the expences of the war, was every day growing more vigorous and independent. The Thebans, who now began to take the lead in the affairs of Greece, were naturally a hardy and robust people, of slow intellects, and strong constitutions. It was a constant maxim with them, to side either with Athens or Sparta in their mutual contests, and which soever they inclined to, they were generally of weight enough to turn the balance. However, they had hitherto made no other use of that weight than to secure themselves; but the spirit which now appeared among them was first implanted by Pelopidas, their deliverer from the Spartan yoke; but still further carried to its utmost height by Epimanondas,

nondas, who now began to figure in the affairs of Greece.

Epimanondas was one of those few exalted characters, who have scarce any vice, and almost every virtue, to distinguish them from the rest of mankind. Though in the beginning, possessed of every quality necessary for the service of the state, he chose to lead a private life, employed in the study of philosophy, and shewing an example of the most rigid observance of all its doctrines. Truly a philosopher, and poor out of taste, he despised riches, without affecting any reputation from that contempt; and, if Justin may be credited, he coveted glory as little as he did money. It was always against his will that commands were conferred upon him; and he behaved himself, when invested with them, in such a manner as did more honour to dignities, than dignities did to him. Fond of leisure, which he devoted to the study of philosophy, he shunned public employments, and made no interest but to be excluded from them. His moderation concealed him so well, that he lived obscure, and almost unknown. His merit, however, discovered him at last. He was taken from his solitude by force, to be placed at the head of armies; and he demonstrated, that philosophy, though generally held in contempt with those who aspire at the glory of arms, is wonderfully useful in forming heroes; for it was, in his opinion, a great advance towards conquering an enemy, to know how to conquer ourselves.

Such was the general appointed to command the Theban army, and act in conjunction with Pelopidas. The Thebans being left out in the general treaty of peace, and thus having the Spartans and Athenians against them, they appeared under the utmost consternation, and all Greece looked upon them as lost and undone. Nothing now remained on both sides but to prepare for action. Epimanondas immediately raised all the troops he could, and began his march; but his army did not amount to six thousand men, while the enemy had above four times that number.

The two armies met at Leuctra, and drew up on a plain. Cleombrotus was upon the right, at the head of a body consisting of Lacedæmonians, in whom he confided most, and whose files were twelve deep, to take the advantage, which his superiority of horse gave him in an open country. Archidamus, the son of Agesilaus, was at the head of the allies, who formed the left wing.

Epimanondas, who resolved to charge with his left, which he commanded in person, strengthened it with the choice of his heavy armed troops, whom he drew up fifty deep; the sacred battalion was upon his left, and closed the wing; the rest of his infantry were posted upon his right, in an oblique line, which, the farther it extended, was the more distant from the enemy. By this uncommon disposition, his design was to cover his flank on the right; to keep off his right wing, as a kind of reserved body, that he might not hazard the event of the

battle

battle upon the weakest part of his army. He was assured that, if he could penetrate the Lacedæmonian phalanx, the rest of the army would soon be put to the rout.

The action began with the cavalry. As the Thebans were better mounted, and braver troops than the Lacedæmonian horse, the latter were not long before they were broken, and driven upon the infantry, which they put into some confusion. Epimanondas following his horse close, marched swiftly up to Cleombrotus, and fell upon his phalanx with all the weight of his heavy battalion. The latter, to make a diversion, detached a body of troops, with orders to take Epimanondas in flank, and to surround him. Pelopidas upon sight of that movement, advanced with incredible speed and boldness, at the head of the Sacred Battalion, to prevent the enemy's design, and flanked Cleombrotus himself, who, by that sudden and unexpected attack, was put into disorder. The battle was very fierce and obstinate; and, whilst Cleombrotus could act, the victory continued in suspence, and declared for neither party. But when he fell dead with his wounds, the Thebans, to complete the victory, and the Lacedæmonians, to avoid the shame of abandoning the body of their king, redoubled their efforts, and a great slaughter ensued on both sides. The Spartans fought with so much fury about the body, that at length they gained their point, and carried it off. Animated by so glorious an advantage, they proposed to return to the charge, which would, perhaps, have proved
successful,

succefsful had the allies feconded their ardour ; but the left wing, feeing the Lacedæmonian phalanx broken, and believing all loft, especially when they heard that the king was dead, took to flight, and drew off the reft of the army. Epimanondas followed them vigoroufly, and killed a great number in the purfuit. The Thebans remained mafters of the field of battle, erected a trophy, and permitted the enemy to bury their dead.

The Lacedæmonians had never received fuch a blow : the moft bloody defeat, till then, had fcarce ever coft them more than four or five hundred of their citizens ; here they loft four thoufand men, of whom one thoufand were Lacedæmonians, and four hundred Spartans, out of feven hundred who were in the battle. The Thebans had only three hundred men killed, among whom were four of their citizens.

So great a victory was followed with inftantaneous effects : numbers of the Grecian ftates, who had hitherto remained neuter, now declared in favour of the conquerors, and encreafed their army to the amount of 70,000 men. Epimanondas entered Laconia with an army, the twelfth part of which were not Thebans ; and finding a country hitherto untouched by an enemy, he ran through it with fire and fword, deftroying and plundering, as far as the river Eurotas.

In the mean time, the Spartans, ftruck with confternation at their late defeat, applied to the Athenians for fuccour, who, after fome hefitation, determined to affift them with all their forces; and a slight advantage the Spartans had gained over the Thebans, in which they did not lose a man, gave a promising dawn of success. The war was then carried on with unabating vigour on both sides. The Theban troops were headed by their favourite general Epaminondas; those of Sparta by Agesilaus, the only man in Greece that was then able to oppose him.

Epaminondas, having failed in an attack upon Sparta, was resolved, before he laid down his command, which was now nearly expiring, to endeavour to effect something that might compensate for his failure. In order to protect Sparta, Agesilaus had withdrawn all the troops from Mantinea; thither, therefore, Epaminondas resolved to bend his course. Being determined to attack the town, he dispatched a troop of horse to view its situation, and to clear the fields of stragglers; but just before they had reached Mantinea, an army of six thousand Athenian auxiliaries arrived by sea, who, without taking any refreshment to their men or horses, rushed out without the city, and attacked and defeated the Theban horse. In the mean time, Epaminondas was advancing with his whole army, with the enemy close upon his rear. Finding it impossible to accomplish his purpose, before he would be overtaken, he determined to halt and give them battle. He had now got within a short way of the town, which has had the honour of giving its name to the conflict of that day—a conflict, the most splendid and best contested, that ever figured in the history of any country.

The Greeks had never fought among themselves with more numerous armies: the Lacedæmonians consisted of more than twenty thousand foot, and two thousand horse; the Thebans, of thirty thousand foot, and three thousand horse. The Theban general marched in the same order of battle, in which he intended to fight, that he might not be obliged, when he came up with the enemy, to lose, in disposing of his army, a precious time that cannot be recovered.

He did not march directly, and with his front to the enemy, but in a column upon the hills, with his left wing foremost, as if he did not intend to fight that day. When he was opposite to them, at a quarter of a league's distance, he made the troops halt, and lay down their arms, as if he designed to encamp there. The enemy, in effect, were deceived by his stand; and, reckoning no longer upon a battle, they quitted their arms, dispersed themselves about the camp, and suffered that ardor to be extinguished, which a near approach of a battle is accustomed to kindle in the hearts of soldiers.

Epimanondas, however, by suddenly wheeling his troops to the right, having changed his column into a line, and having drawn out the choice troops, whom he had in his march posted in front, made them double their files upon the front of his left wing, to add to its strength, and to put it into a condition to attack in point

the

the Lacedæmonian phalanx, which, by the movement he had made, faced it directly. He ordered the center and right wing of his army to move very slowly, and to halt before they came up with the enemy, that he might not hazard the event of the battle upon troops, of whom he had no great opinion.

He expected to decide the victory by that body of chosen troops, which he commanded in person, and which he had formed into a column to attack the enemy in a wedge-like point. He had persuaded himself, that if he could penetrate the Lacedæmonian phalanx, in which the enemy's principal force consisted, he should not find it difficult to rout the rest of the army, by charging upon the right and left with his victorious troops. After having disposed his whole army in this manner, he moved on to charge the enemy with the whole weight of his column. They were strangely surprised when they saw Epimanondas advance to them in this order, and resumed their arms, bridled their horses, and made all the haste they could to their ranks.

Whilst Epimanondas marched against the enemy, the cavalry that covered his flank, on the left, the best at that time in Greece, entirely composed of Thebans and Thessalians, had orders to attack the enemy's horse. The Theban general, whom nothing escaped, had artfully bestowed bowmen in the intervals of his horse, in order to begin the disorders of the enemy's cavalry, by a previous discharge of a shower of arrows, stones, and javelins upon
them

them. The other army had neglected to take the same precaution; and had been guilty of another fault, not less considerable, in giving as much depth to the squadrons as if they had been a phalanx. By these means, their horse were incapable of supporting long the charge of the Thebans; and, after having made several ineffectual attacks with great loss, they were obliged to retire behind their infantry.

Epimanondas, in the mean time, with his body of foot, had charged the Lacedæmonian phalanx. The troops fought on both sides with incredible ardor, both the Thebans and Lacedæmonians being resolved to perish, rather than yield the glory of arms to their rivals. They began with fighting their spears; but these being soon broken in the fury of the combat, they charged each other sword in hand. The resistance was equally obstinate, and the slaughter very great on both sides. The troops despising danger, and desiring only to distinguish themselves by the greatness of their actions, chose rather to die in their ranks, than to lose a step of their ground.

The furious slaughter on both sides having continued a great while, without the victory inclining to either, Epimanondas to force it to declare for him, thought it his duty to make an extraordinary effort in person, without regard to the danger of his own life. He formed, therefore, a troop of the bravest and most determinate about him; and, putting himself at the head of them, made a vigorous charge upon the enemy, where the battle was most warm, and wounded the Lacedæmonian general with the first javelin he threw. The troops, by his example, having wounded or killed all that stood in their way, broke and penetrated the phalanx. The Lacedæmonians dismayed by the presence of Epimanondas, and overpowered by the weight of that intrepid party, were reduced to give ground. The gross of the Theban troops, animated by their general's example and success, drove back the enemy upon his right and left and made great slaughter of them. But some of the Spartan troops, perceiving that Epimanondas abandoned himself too much to his ardour, suddenly rallied, and, returning to the fight, charged him with a shower of javelins. Whilst he kept off part of those darts, shunned some of them, fenced off others, and was fighting with the most heroic valour, to assure the victory to his army, a Spartan, named Callicrates, gave him a mortal wound with a javelin in his breast, across his cuiras. The wood of the javelin being broken off, and the iron head continuing in the wound, the torment was insupportable, and he fell immediately.—The battle begun around him with new fury, the one side using their utmost endeavours to take him alive, and the other to save him.—The Thebans gained their point at last, and carried him off, after having put the enemy to flight.

After several different movements, and alternate losses and disadvantages, the troops on both sides stood still, and rested upon their arms;

The Death of Epaminondas.

arms; when the trumpets of the two armies, as if by consent, sounded the retreat at the same time. Each party pretended to the victory, and erected a trophy: the Thebans, because they had defeated the right wing, and remained masters of the field of battle; and the Athenians, because they had cut the general's detachment in pieces.— From this point of honour, both sides at first refused to ask leave to bury their dead, which with the ancients, was confessing their defeat. The Lacedæmonians, however, sent to demand that permission; after which, the rest had no thoughts, but of paying the last duties to the slain.

In the mean time, Epimanondas had been carried into the camp. The surgeons, after having examined the wound, declared, that he would expire as soon as the head of the dart was drawn out of it. These words gave all that were present the utmost sorrow and affliction, who were inconsolable on seeing so great a man on the point of death. For him, the only concern he expressed was about his arms, and the fate of the battle. When they shewed him his shield, and assured him, that the Thebans had gained the victory, turning towards his friends with a serene and calm air, "All then is well," said he; and soon after, upon drawing the head of the javelin out of his body, he expired in the arms of victory.

As the glory of Thebes rose with Epimanondas, so it fell with him; and he is perhaps, the only, instance of one man being able to inspire his country with military glory, and lead it to conquest, without having had a predecessor, or leaving an imitator of his example.

The battle of Mantinea was the greatest that was ever fought by Grecians against Grecians, the whole strength of the country being drawn out, and ranged according to their different interests; and it was fought with an obstinacy equal to the importance of it, which was the fixing the empire of Greece, which must of course have been transferred to the Thebans, upon their victory, if they had not lost the fruits of it by the death of their general, who was the soul of all their counsels and designs. This blasted all their hopes, and put out their sudden blaze of power almost as soon as it was kindled. However, they did not presently give up their pretensions; they were still ranked among the leading states, and made several further struggles; but they were faint and ineffectual, and such as were rather for life and being, than for superiority and dominion. A peace, therefore, was proposed, which was ratified by all the states of Greece, except Sparta: the conditions of which were, that every state should maintain what they possessed, and hold it independent of any other power. A state of repose followed this peace, in which the Grecian powers seemed to slacken from their former animosities, and there was little done for several years following.

CHAP.

CHAP. VI.

DURING these transactions, a power was growing up in Greece, hitherto unobserved, but now too conspicuous and formidable to be overlooked in the general picture: this was that of the Macedonians; a people hitherto obscure, and in a manner barbarous; and who, though warlike and courageous, had never yet presumed to intermeddle in the affairs of Greece. Now several circumstances concurred to raise them from that obscurity, and to involve them in measures, which, by degrees, wrought a thorough change in the state of Greece.

This state began to make a figure about the beginning of the ninety-sixth Olympiad. Philip, the father of Alexander the Great, who had been the pupil of Epimanondas, was no sooner become king of Macedon, than he began to distinguish himself. He succeeded in every thing he undertook, by the artfulness of his address, and the force of his eloquence, of which he was a great master.— He first gained the affections of his subjects, then trained and exercised them, and reformed their discipline. It was at this time he instituted the famous Macedonian phalanx, which did so much execution. It was an improvement upon the ancient manners of fighting among the Grecians, who generally drew up their foot so close, as to stand the shock of the

enemy

enemy without being broken. The complete phalanx was thought to contain above sixteen thousand men; but this of Philip's invention is described by Polybius to be an oblong figure, consisting of eight thousand pikemen, sixteen deep, and five hundred in front, the men standing so close together, that the pikes of the fifth rank were extended three feet beyond the line of the front. The rest, whose distance from the front rendered their pikes of less, rested them upon the shoulders of those who stood before them, and so locking them together in file, pressed forward to support and push on the former ranks, whereby the assault was rendered more violent and irresistible.

Philip having, by some means or other, set the Greeks to quarrelling among themselves, thought it his interest to remain neuter in the commotions he had partly occasioned. It was consistent with the ambitious policy of this prince to be intent only upon his own interest, and not to engage in a war, by which he could reap not the least benefit; and to take advantage of a juncture, in which all Greece, employed and divided by a great war, gave him an opportunity to extend his frontiers, and push his conquests, without any apprehensions of opposition. He was also well pleased to see both parties weaken and consume each other, as he should thereby be enabled to fall upon them afterwards to greater advantage.

Philip, as soon as his son Alexander was born, lost no time in acquainting Aristotle of what had happened. He wrote to that distinguished gnished philosopher, in terms the most polite and flattering; begging of him to come and undertake his education, and to bestow on him those useful lessons of magnanimity and virtue, which every great man ought to possess, and which his numerous avocations rendered impossible to be attempted by him. He added, " I return thanks to the Gods, not so much for having given me a son, as for having given him to me in the age in which Aristole lives."

Though brevity will not permit us to follow every method Philip took to enslave all Greece, yet we must not omit to mention a circumstance that happened at the siege of Methone, where Philip lost one of his eyes in a very singular manner. After of Amphipolis had offered his services to Philip, telling him, that he was so excellent a markfman, that he could bring down birds in their most rapid flight. The monarch made this answer: " Well, I will take you into my service, when I make war upon starlings;" which answer stung the archer to the quick. A repartee proves often of fatal consequence to him who makes it. After, having thrown himself into the city, let fly an arrow, on which was written," To Philip's left eye." This carried a most cruel proof that he was a good markfman, for he hit him in the right eye; and Philip sent him back the same arrow, with this inscription, " If Philip takes the city, he will hang up After;" and accordingly he was as good as his word. A skilful surgeon drew the arrow out of Philip's eye with so much art and dexterity, that not the least

fear

fear remained; and though he could not save his eye, yet he took away the blemish.

The hasty strides Philip was now making towards enslaving all Greece, particularly attracted the attention of Demosthenes, who roused the Athenians from their lethargy of pleasure. This celebrated orator saw, from the beginning, the ambition of Philip, and the power, of which he was possessed to carry him through his designs. This illustrious orator and statesmen was born in the last year of the ninety-ninth Olympiad. He was the son of an eminent Athenian citizen, who raised a considerable fortune by the manufacture of arms. At the age of seven years, he lost his father; and, to add to this misfortune, the guardians, to whom he was entrusted, wasted and embezzled a considerable part of his inheritance. Thus oppressed by fraud, and discouraged by a weak and effeminate habit of body, he yet discovered an early ambition to distinguish himself as a popular speaker. His first essay was made against his guardian, by whom he had been so injuriously treated; but the goodness of his cause was here of more service than the abilities of the young orator: for his early attempts were unpromising. He twice afterwards attempted to harrangue the people; but he succeeded so badly, that they even hissed him, when he went away ashamed, confounded, and quite in despair.

After a length of time, however, after proper instructions, and unwearied application, he appeared again in public, and succeeded so well,
that

that people flocked from all parts of Greece to hear him. From thence he was looked upon as the standard of true eloquence, insomuch that none of his countrymen have been put in comparison with him, nor even among the Romans, any but Cicero. His eloquence was grave and austere, like his temper; masculine and sublime, bold, forcible, and impetuous; abounding with metaphors, apostrophes, and interrogations, which, with his solemn way of invoking and appealing to the gods, the planets, the elements, and the manes of those who fell at Salamis and Marathon, had such a wonderful effect upon his hearers, that they thought him inspired. But Demosthenes could not have made such impressions on them, if his talent of speaking had not been supported by their opinion of his integrity. It was that which added weight and emphasis to every thing he said, and animated the whole; it was that which chiefly engaged their attention, and determined their councils, when they were convinced he spoke from his heart and had no interest to manage but that of the community. Of this he gave the strongest proof in his zeal against Philip, who said he was of more weight against him than all the fleets and armies of the Athenians, and that he had no enemy but Demosthenes. He was not wanting in his endeavours to corrupt him, as he had done most of the leading men in Greece; but this great orator withstood all his efforts; and as it was observed, all the gold in Macedon could not bribe him.

Though Philip's public character was by no means a credit to him, yet the following act of private justice does him honour. A certain soldier in the Macedonian army had, in many instances, distinguished himself by extraordinary acts of valour, and had received many marks of Philip's favour and approbation. On some occasion, he embarked on board a vessel, which was wrecked in a violent storm, he himself cast on the shore helpless and naked, and scarcely with the appearance of life. A Macedonian, whose lands were contiguous to the sea, came opportunely to be witness of his distress, and with all humane and charitable tenderness, flew to the relief of the unhappy stranger. He bore him to his house, laid him in his own bed, revived, cherished, comforted, and for forty days supplied him freely with all the necessaries and conveniences, which his languishing condition could require. The soldier, thus happily rescued from death, was incessant in the warmest expressions of gratitude to his benefactor, assured him of his interest with the king, and of his power and resolution of obtaining for him, from the royal bounty, the noble returns which such extraordinary benevolence had merited. He was now completely recovered, and his kind host supplied him with money to pursue his journey.

Some time after, the soldier presented himself before the king; he recounted his misfortunes, magnified his services, and, having looked with an eye of envy on the possessions of the man who had preserved his life, was now so abandoned

doned to every sense of gratitude, as to request the king to bestow upon him the house and lands where he had been so kindly and tenderly entertained. Unhappily, Philip, without examination, inconsiderately and precipitately granted his infamous request. This soldier now returned to his preserver, repaid his goodness by driving him from his settlement, and taking immediate possession of all the fruits of his honest industry. The poor man, stung with this instance of unparalleled ingratitude and insensibility, boldly determined, instead of submitting to his wrongs, to seek relief; and, in a letter addressed to Philip, represented his own and the soldier's conduct, in a lively and affecting manner. The king was instantly fired with indignation, and ordered that justice should be done without delay; that the possessions should be immediately restored to the man, whose charitable offices had been thus horribly repaid; and, having seized the soldier, caused these words to be branded on his forehead. "The Ungrateful Guest:" a character infamous in every age, and among all nations; but particularly among the Greeks, who, from the earliest times, were most scrupulously observant of the laws of hospitality.

Philip, having proved unsuccessful in his attacks on the Grecian States, marched against Atheus, king of Scythia, from whom he had received some personal cause of discontent, and took his son Alexander with him in this expedition. Though the Scythians had a very numerous army, he defeated them without any

difficulty

difficulty. He got a very great booty, which consisted not in gold or silver, the use of which the Scythians were not as yet so unhappy as to know, but in cattle, in horses, and in a great number of women and children.

At his return from Scythia, the Triballi, a people of Moesia, disputed the pass with him, laying claim to part of the plunder he was carrying off. Philip was forced to come to a battle; and a very bloody one was fought, in which great numbers on each side were killed upon the spot. The king himself was wounded in the thigh, and, with the same thrust, had his horse killed under him. Alexander flew to his father's aid, and, covering him with his shield, killed or put to flight all who attacked him.

The ambition of Philip would not long suffer him to remain inactive. Not daring openly to attack the Athenians, he endeavoured, underhand, to create new disturbances in Greece, that he might take such a part in them as would best answer his views; and when the flame should be kindled, his point was to appear rather to be called in as an assistant, than to act as a principal.

However, the mask was soon thrown off: the Thebans and Athenians soon joined their forces, and waited the approach of Philip, who was leading his army to the plain of Chæronea: a name rendered famous by the event of this important contest. Philip's army was formed of thirty-two thousand men, warlike, disciplined, and long enured to the toils and dangers of the field; but this body was composed of different

nations

Alexander covering his father with his Shield.

nations and countries, who had each their distinct and separate views and interests. The army of the confederates did not amount to thirty thousand complete, of which the Athenians and Thebans furnished the greater part; the rest was formed of the Corinthians and Peloponnesians; but the same motives, and the same zeal, influenced and animated them. All were equally effected by the event, and all equally resolved to conquer, or die in defence of their liberty.

The fatal morning now arrived, which was for ever to decide the cause of liberty, and the empire of Greece. Before the rising of the sun, both armies were ranged in order of battle. The Thebans, commanded by Theogenes, a man of but moderate abilities in war, and suspected of corruption, obtained the post of honor on the right wing of the confederate Greeks, with that famous body in the front, called the Sacred Band, formed of generous and warlike youths, connected and endeared to each other by all the noble enthusiasm of love and friendship. The centre was formed of the Corinthians and Peloponnesians, and the Athenians composed the left wing, led by their generals Lysicles and Chares. On the left of the Macedonian army stood Alexander, at the head of a chosen body of noble Macedonians, supported by the famous cavalry of Thessaly. As this prince was then but nineteen years old, his father was careful to curb his youthful impetuosity, and to direct his valour, and for this purpose surrounded him with a number of experienced officers. In the centre were placed those Greeks who had united with Philip, and on whose courage he had the least dependence; while the king himself commanded on the right wing, where his renowned phalanx stood, to oppose the impetuosity, with which the Athenians were well known to begin their onset.

The charge, begun on each side with all the courage and violence, which ambition, revenge, the love of glory, and the love of liberty, could excite in the several combatants. Alexander, at the head of the Macedonian nobles, with all the fury of youthful courage, first fell on the Sacred Band of Thebes, which sustained his attack with a bravery and vigour worthy of its former fame. The gallant youths who composed this body, not being timely, or not duly supported by their countrymen, bore up for a while against the torrent of the enemy; till at length, oppressed and overpowered by superior numbers, without yielding or turning their backs on their assailants, they sunk down on that ground where they had been originally stationed, each by the side of his darling friend, raising up a bulwark by their bodies against the progress of the enemy. The young Alexander and his forces, in all the enthusiastic ardour of valour, animated by success, pushed on through all the carnage, over all the heaps of slain, and fell furiously on the main body of the Thebans, where they were opposed with obstinate and deliberate courage; and the contest was, for some time, supported with mutual violence.

At

At the same time, the Athenians, on the right wing, fought with a spirit and intrepidity worthy of the character which they boasted, and of the cause by which they were animated. Many brave efforts were exerted on each side, and success was for some time doubtful; till at length, part of the center, and the left wing of the Macedonians, except the phalanx, yielded to the impetuous attack of the Athenians, and fled with some precipitation. Happy had it been on that day for Greece, if the conduct and abilities of the Grecian generals had been equal to the valour of their soldiers; but these brave champions of liberty were led on by the despicable creatures of intrigue and cabal.—Transported by the advantage now obtained, the presumptuous Lysicles cried out, "Come on, my gallant countrymen, the victory is ours; let us pursue these cowards, and drive them to Macedon." Thus, instead of improving the happy opportunity, by charging the phalanx in flank, and so breaking that formidable body, the Athenians wildly and precipitately pressed forward, in pursuit of the flying enemy, themselves in all the disorder and tumult of a rout.

Philip saw this fatal error with all the contempt of a skilful general, and the secret exultation arising from the assurance of approaching victory. He cooly observed to the officers that stood round him, that the Athenians knew not how to conquer. He ordered the phalanx to change its position, and, by a sudden evolution, to gain possession of an adjacent eminence. From thence they marched deliberately down, firm and collected, and fell, with their united force, on the Athenians, now confident of success, and blind to their danger. The shock was irresistible, they were at once overwhelmed, many of them lay crushed by the weight of the enemy, and expiring by their wounds; while the rest escaped from the dreadful slaughter by a shameful and precipitate flight, bearing down, and hurrying away with them, those troops that had been stationed for their support. Now Demosthenes, that renowned orator and statesman, whose noble sentiments and spirited harangues had raised the courage on this day so eminently excited, betrayed that weakness which has sullied his great character. He alone, of all his countrymen, advanced to the charge cold and dismayed; and, on the very first appearance of a reverse of fortune, in an agony of terror, turned his back, cast away that shield, which he had adorned with this inscription, in golden characters, "To Good Fortune," and appeared the foremost in the general rout. The ridicule and malice of his enemies related, or perhaps invented, another shameful circumstance; being impeded in his flight by some brambles, his imagination was so possessed by the presence of an enemy, that he loudly cried out for quarter.

While Philip was thus triumphant on his side, Alexander continued the conflict on the other wing, and at length broke the Thebans, in spite of all their acts of valor, who now fled from the field, and were pursued with great carnage. The center of the confederates was

thus

thus totally abandoned to the fury of a victorious enemy. But slaughter enough had been already made; more than one thousand of the Athenians lay dead on the field of battle, two thousand were made prisoners, and the loss of the Thebans was not inferior. Philip, therefore, determined to conclude his important victory by an act of apparent clemency, which his ambition and policy really dictated. He gave orders that the Greeks should be spared, conscious of his own designs, and still expecting to appear in the field the head and leader of that body, which he had now completely conquered.

This defeat was attributed chiefly to the ill conduct of the generals Lysicles and Chares; the former whereof the Athenians put to death at the instance of a judge, named Lycurgus, who had great credit and influence with the people, but was a severe judge, and a most bitter accuser. "You, Lysicles, (said he) were general of the army: a thousand citizens were slain, and two thousand taken prisoners; a trophy has been erected to the dishonour of this city, and all Greece is enslaved. You had the command when all these things happened; and yet you dare to live, to view the light of the sun, and blush not to appear publicly in the forum: you, Lysicles, who are born the monument of your country's shame!" It does not appear that Chares underwent any kind of persecution for his share of this action; though, according to his general character, he deserved it more than his colleague; he had no talent for command, and was very little different

from

from a common soldier. Timotheus said of him, that, "instead of being a general, he was fitter to carry the general's baggage."

After the battle of Chæronea, such orators as opposed Demosthenes, having all risen up in concert against him, and having cited him to take his trial according to law, the people not only declared him innocent of the several accusations laid to his charge, but conferred on him additional honors.

Philip, however, did not long enjoy the fruits of his conquests in Greece. Pausanias, a young Macedonian nobleman, having received a most shameful insult from Attilus, a relation of Philip's, he applied to the monarch for redress; but not being able to obtain it, he resolved on the destruction of Philip. Pausanias chose the morning in which was to be a grand procession, for the execution of his revenge on the prince, who had denied reparation to his injured honor. His design had been for some time premeditated, and now was the dreadful moment of effecting it. As Philip marched on in all his pride and pomp, this young Macedonian slipped through the crowd, and, with a desperate and revengeful resolution, waited his approach in a narrow passage, just at the entrance into the theatre. The king advanced towards him, Pausanias drew his poniard, plunged it into his heart, and the conqueror of Greece, and the terror of Asia, fell prostrate to the ground, and instantly expired.

The murderer flew towards the gates of the city, where there stood horses to favor his
escape,

escape, which Olympias, Philip's wife, is said
to have prepared. Here it should be observed,
that Philip had disgraced Olympias, for her
bad and disagreeable temper, and had taken
Cleopatra to his bed. The tumult and confusion was such as might be expected from so
fatal an event: some of the Macedonians
crowded round the fallen king with officious
and ineffectual care, while others pursued Pausanias. Among these were Perdiccas, Attalus,
and Leonatus, who coming up with him just as
he was preparing to remount his horse, from
which he had been thrown by his foot tangling
in a vine, they fell upon him, and dispatched
him. His body was immediately hung on a
gibbet; but, in the morning, it appeared
crowned with a golden diadem: the only means
by which Olympias could express her implaca-
ble resentment. In a few days, indeed, she
took a further occasion of publishing her triumph and exultation in her husband's fall, by
paying the same funeral honors to Pausanias,
which was prepared for Philip: both bodies
were burnt on the same pile, and the ashes of
both deposited in the same tomb. She is even
said to have prevailed on the Macedonians to
pay annual honors to Pausanias; as if she
feared, that the share she had taken in the death
of Philip should not be sufficiently known to
the world. She consecrated to Apollo the dagger, which had been the instrument of the fatal
deed, inscribed with the name Myrtalis, the
name which she had borne when their loves first

began.

began. Thus died Philip, whose virtues and vices were directed and proportioned to his ambition.

CHAP. VIII.

IN the year of the world 3648, and 356 before the birth of Christ, Alexander, the son of Philip, ascended the throne of Macedon, and took possession of a kingdom rendered flourishing and powerful by the policy of the preceding reign. Alexander, upon his accession to the throne, saw himself surrounded with extreme dangers; the barbarous nations, with whom Philip contended during his whole reign, thought this change for their advantage; and, despising the youth and inexperience of the young monarch, resolved to seize this opportunity of regaining their freedom. Nor had he less to fear from the Greeks themselves, who now thought this a convenient opportunity to restore their ancient form of government, revenge their former injuries, and reclaim those rights they had enjoyed for ages. Alexander, however, resolved to prevent their machinations, and to give them no time to complete their confederacies against him. He made all possible haste to check the arms of the barbarians, by marching his troops to the banks of the Danube, which he crossed in one night.— He defeated the king of the Triballi in a great battle, made the Getæ fly at his approach, and

subdued

subdued several other barbarous nations, some by the terror of his name, and others by the force of his arms.

The first object of Alexander's ambition was the conquest of Persia: and he now expected, that he should have leisure and opportunity to prepare for so great an enterprize. He was however, soon called to a new undertaking; for the Athenians, Thebans, and Lacedæmonians, united against him, hoping by the assistance of Persia, to recover their freedom. Expedition and activity were the characteristics of Alexander. Having heard of the union formed against him by the Grecian States, he crossed over the craggy top of Mount Ossa, to elude the Thessalonians, who had possessed themselves of the defiles lying between Thessaly and Macedon; and moved on with such rapidity, that his appearance in Greece gave the first news of his preparation for war. A great battle was soon fought, in which the Thebans exerted themselves with a bravery and ardour much above their strength; but they were at last surrounded on all sides, the greatest part of them were cut to pieces, and the city taken, plundered and destroyed. However, he set at liberty the priests; all such as had a right of hospitality with the Macedonians; the descendants of Pindar, the famous poet, who had done so much to Greece; and such as had opposed the revolt: but all the rest, in number about thirty thousand, he sold; and upwards of six thousand had been killed in battle.

This dreadful example of severity towards so powerful a city as Thebes, spread the terror of his arms through all Greece, and made all things give way before him. He summoned at Corinth the assemblies of the several states and free cities of Greece, to obtain from them the same supreme command against the Persians, which had been granted to his father a little before his death. No assembly ever debated on a more important subject: it was the western world deliberating upon the ruin of the east, and the method for executing a revenge which had been suspended for more than an age. The assembly held at this time gave rise to events, the relation of which will appear astonishing, and almost incredible; and to revolutions, which contributed to change the disposition of most things in the political world. The deliberations of the assembly were short: the Spartans were the only people who ventured to remonstrate; though several others were inimical to the interests of the Macedonians; but they were forced to submit, and Alexander was appointed generalissimo against the Persians.

Having thus far accomplished his wishes, and after having completely settled his affairs in Macedonia, he set out for Asia in the beginning of the spring. His army consisted of little more than thirty thousand foot, and four or five thousand horse; but they were all brave men, well disciplined, and enured to fatigue. They had made several campaigns under Philip, and were each of them, in case of necessity, capable of commanding. Most of the officers were

near

near three-score years of age, and the common men fifty; and when they were either assembled, or drawn up at the head of a camp, they had the air of a venerable senate. Such was the army that was to decide the fortune, not only of Greece, but of all the eastern world.

When the news of Alexander's landing in Asia, without opposition, was brought to Darius, he testified the utmost contempt for the Macedonian army, and indignation at the presumption of their generals. In a letter which he wrote, he reprehended his audacious insolence, and gave orders to his various governors, in the different parts of his dominions, that, if they took Alexander alive, to whip him with rods, make prisoners of his whole army, and send them as slaves to one of the most deserted parts of his dominions. Thus confiding in the glittering but barbarous multitude he commanded, he disposed of the enemy as already vanquished; but confidence goes but a short part of the road to success. The great numbers he had gathered only brought unwieldy splendor into the field, and, instead of procuring him security, encreased his embarrassments.

Alexander, in the mean time, marched on at the head of his heavy-armed infantry, drawn up in two lines, with the cavalry in the wings, and the baggage following in the rear. Being arrived on the banks of the Granicus, he there found the Persian horse, which were very numerous, on the opposite shore, forming a large front, in order to oppose Alexander, whenever he should attempt to pass. The two

armies

armies continued a long time in sight of each
other, on the banks of the river, as if dreading the event. The Persians waited till the
Macedonians should enter the river, in order to
charge them to advantage upon their landing;
and the latter seemed to be making choice of a
place proper for landing.

At last, Alexander ordered his horse to be
brought, commanded the noblemen of the
court to follow him and behave gallantly. He
himself commanded the right wing, and Parmenio the left. The king first caused a strong
detachment to march into the river, himself
following it with the rest of the forces. He
made Parmenio advance afterwards with the
left wing, the trumpet sounding, and the whole
army raising cries of joy. The Persians, seeing
this detachment advance forward, began to let
fly their arrows, and march to a place where
the declivity was not so great, in order to keep
the Macedonians from landing. But now the
horse engaged with great fury, one part endeavouring to land, and the other striving to prevent them. The Macedonians, whose cavalry
were inferior in number, besides the disadvantage of the ground, were wounded with the
darts that were shot from the eminence; not to
mention, that the flower of the Persian horse
were drawn together in this place. The Macedonians, therefore, at first gave ground, after
having lost the first ranks, which made a vigorous defence. Alexander, who closely followed
them, reinforced them with his best troops,
headed them himself, animated them by his
presence

presence, pushed the Persians, and routed them; upon which the whole army followed after, crossed the river, and attacked the enemy on all sides.

Spithrobates, lieutenant-governor of Ionia, and son-in-law to Darius, distinguished himself above the rest of the Persian generals by his superior bravery. Being surrounded by forty Persian lords, all of them his relations, of experienced valor, and who never moved from his side, he carried terror wherever he went. Alexander observing in how gallant a manner he signalized himself, clapt spurs to his horse, and advanced towards him. They immediately engaged, and each having thrown a javelin, wounded the other slightly. Spithrobates fell furiously sword in hand upon Alexander, who, being prepared for him, thrusts his pike into his face, and laid him dead at his feet. At that very moment Rasaces, brother to that nobleman, charging him on the side, gave him so furious a blow on the head with a battle-axe, that he beat off his plume, but went no deeper than the hair. As he was going to repeat his blow on the head, which now appeared through his fractured helmet, Clitus cut off Rasaces' hand with one stroke of his scimitar, and thereby saved his sovereign's life. The danger to which Alexander had been exposed, greatly animated the courage of his soldiers, who now performed wonders. The Persians in the center of the horse, upon whom the light-armed troops, who had been posted in the intervals of the horse, poured a perpetual discharge of darts, being

unable

unable any longer to sustain the attack of the Macedonians, who struck them all in the face, the two wings were immediately broken, and put to flight. Alexander did not long pursue them, but immediately turned about to charge the foot. These at first stood their ground; but when they saw themselves attacked at the same time by the cavalry, and the Macedonian phalanx which had crossed the river, and that the battalions were now engaged, those of the Persians did not make either a long or a vigorous defence, and were soon put to flight; but the Grecian infantry in Darius' service stood the shock. This body of foot retiring to a hill, demanded a promise from Alexander to let them march away unmolested; but following the dictates of his wrath, rather than those of reason, he rushed into the midst of this body of foot, and presently lost his horse, which was killed by the thrust of a sword. The battle was so hot round him, that most of the Macedonians, who lost their lives on this occasion, fell here; for they fought against a body of men, who were well disciplined, had been inured to war, and fought in despair. They were all cut to pieces, except two thousand, who were taken prisoners.

In this battle twenty thousand foot, and two thousand five hundred horse, were killed on the side of the barbarians; and of the Macedonians, twenty five of the royal horse were killed on the first attack. Alexander ordered Lysippus to make their statues in brass, all of which were set up in a city of Macedon, called Dia,

from

from whence they were many years afterwards carried to Rome by Metelles. About threescore of the other horse were killed, and near thirty foot, who, the next day, were all laid with their arms and equipage in one grave; and the king granted an exemption to their fathers and children from every kind of tribute and service. This victory not only impressed the Persians with consternation, but served to excite the ardour of the invading army.

Soon after the battle of Grannicus, he recovered Sardis from the enemy, which was in a manner the bulwark of the barbarian empire. Four days after, he arrived at Ephesus, carrying with him those who had been banished from thence for being his adherents, and restored its popular form of government.

Alexander afterwards took Miletus, and demolished Halicarnassus to the very foundation. He next restored Ada, queen of Caria, to her kingdom, of which she had been dispossessed some time before; and as a testimony of the deep sense she had of the favours received from Alexander, she sent him every day meats dressed in the most exquisite manner, and the most excellent cooks of every kind. Alexander answered the queen upon this occasion, that all this train was of no service to him; for that he was possessed of much better cooks, whom Leonidas his governor had given him; one of whom prepared him a good dinner, and the other an excellent supper: these were Temperance and Exercise.

He soon afterwards marched into Phrygia, the ancient dominion of the celebrated king Midas. Having taken the capital city, he was desirous of seeing the famous chariot, to which the gordian knot was tied. This knot, which fastened the yoke to the beam, was tied with so much intricacy, that it was impossible to discover where the ends begun, or how they were concealed. According to an ancient tradition of the country, an oracle had foretold, that the man who could untie it should possess the empire of Asia. Alexander being firmly persuaded that the oracle was meant for him, after many fruitless trials, instead of attempting to untie it in the usual manner, drew his sword, and cut it into pieces, crying out, such was the only way to untie it. The priest hailed the omen, and declared that Alexander fulfilled the oracle.

Darius having been employed, for a long time, in collecting a numerous army to oppose Alexander, advanced towards the river Euphrates. Over his tent was exhibited, to the view of his whole army, the image of the sun in jewels, while wealth and magnificence shone in every quarter of the army. First they carried silver altars, on which lay fire, called by them Sacred and Eternal; and these were followed by the Magi, singing hymns, after the manner of their country. They were accompanied by three hundred and sixty-five youths, equalling the number of days in a year, clothed in purple robes. Afterwards came a chariot consecrated to Jupiter, drawn by white horses, and followed

by

by a courser of prodigious size, to whom they gave the name of the Sun's Horse; and the equerries were dressed in white, each having a golden rod in his hand.

Ten chariots, adorned with sculptures of gold and silver, followed afterwards. Then marched a body of horse, composed of twelve nations, whose manners and customs were various, and all armed in a different manner. Next advanced those, whom the Persians called *The Immortals*, amounting to ten thousand, who surpassed the rest of the barbarians in the sumptuousness of their apparel. They all wore golden collars, were cloathed in robes of gold tissue, with vestments having sleeves to them, quite covered with precious stones. Thirty paces from them, followed those called the king's relations, to the number of fifteen thousand, in habits very much resembling those of women, and more remarkable for the vain pomp of their dress, than the glitter of their arms. Those called the Doryphori came afterwards: they carried the king's cloak, and walked before the chariot, in which he seemed to sit as on a high throne. This chariot was enriched on both sides with images of the gods, in gold and silver; and from the middle of the yoke, which was covered with jewels, rose two statues, a cubit in height, the one representing war, the other peace, having a golden eagle between them, with wings extended, as ready to take flight. But nothing could equal the magnificence of the king; he was cloathed in a vest of purple, striped with silver, and over it hung a long robe, glittering all over with gold and precious stones, that represented two falcons, rushing from the clouds, and pecking at one another. Around his waist he wore a golden girdle, after the manner of women, whence his scimitar hung, the scabbard of which flamed all over with gems. On his head he wore a tiara, or mitre, round which was a fillet of blue mixed with white. On each side of him walked two hundred of his nearest relations, whose pikes were adorned with silver, and tipped with gold; and lastly, thirty thousand infantry, who composed the rear-guard. These were followed by the king's horses, four hundred in number, all which were led.

About one hundred paces from thence, came Sysigambis, the mother of Darius, seated on a chariot, and his consort on another, with the several female attendants of both queens riding on horseback. Afterwards came fifteen large chariots, in which were the king's children, and those who had the care of their education, with a band of eunuchs. Then marched the concubines, to the number of three hundred and sixty, in the equipage of queens, followed by six hundred mules, and three hundred camels, which carried the king's treasure, and guarded by a great body of archers. After these came the wives of the crown-officers, and of the greatest lords of the court; then the sutlers and servants of the army, seated also in chariots. In the rear were a body of light armed troops, with their commanders, who closed the whole march.

Such

Such was the splendour of this pageant monarch: he took the field encumbered with an unnecessary train of concubines, attended with troops of various nations, speaking different languages; from their numbers impossible to be marshalled, and so rich and effeminate in gold and in garments, as seemed rather to invite than deter an enemy.

CHAP. IX.

ALEXANDER, as frequently happens to the greatest captains, felt some emotions, when he saw that he was going to hazard all at once. The more fortune had favoured him hitherto, the more he now dreaded her frowns: the moment was approaching, which was to determine his fate. On the other side, his courage revived from the reflection, that the reward of his toils exceeded the dangers of them; and, though he was uncertain with regard to the victory, he at least hoped to die gloriously, and like Alexander. However, he did not divulge these thoughts to any one, well knowing that, upon the approach of a battle, a general ought not to discover the least marks of sadness or perplexity, and that the troops should read nothing but resolution and intrepidity in the countenance of their commander.

Having made his soldiers refresh themselves, and ordered them to be ready by three o'clock in the morning, he went to the top of a mountain,

tain, and there, by torch light, sacrificed, after the manner of his country, to the gods of the place. As soon as the signal was given, his army, which was ready to march and fight, arrived by day-break at the several posts assigned them. But the spies now bringing word, that Darius was not above thirty furlongs from them the king caused his army to halt, and then drew it up in battle array. The peasants, in the greatest terror, came also, and acquainted Darius with the arrival of the enemy, which he would not at first believe, imagining that Alexander fled before him, and was endeavoring to escape. This news threw his troops into the utmost confusion, who, in their surprise, ran to their arms with great precipitation and disorder.

The spot where the battle was fought, lay near the city of Issus, which the mountains bounded on one side, and the sea on the other. The plain that was situated between them both must have been considerably broad, as the two armies encamped in it. The river Pinarius ran through the middle of this plain, from the mountain to the sea, and divided it very nearly into two equal parts. The mountain formed a hollow kind of gulf, the extremity of which, in a curved line, bounded part of the plain.

Alexander had at first advanced very slowly, to prevent the ranks on the front of the phalanx from breaking, and halted by intervals; but when he was got within bow-shot, he commanded all his right wing to plunge impetuously into the river, purposely that he might surprise the Barbarians, come sooner to a close

engagement,

engagement, and be less exposed to the enemy's
arrows; in all which he was very successful.
Both sides fought with the utmost bravery and
resolution; and, being now forced to fight
close, they charged both sides sword in hand,
when a dreadful slaughter ensued, each enga-
ging man to man. Alexander wished nothing
so ardently as to kill with his own hand
Darius, who, being seated on a high chariot,
was conspicuous to the whole army. Oxathres,
brother to Darius, observing that Alexander
was going to charge that monarch with the utmost vigour, rushed before his chariot with the
horse under his command, and distinguished
himself above the rest. The horses that drew
Darius's chariot lost all command, and shook
the yoke so violently, that they were upon the
point of overturning the king, who, seeing
himself going to fall alive into the hands of his
enemies, leaped down and mounted another
chariot. The rest, observing this, fled as fast
as possible, and throwing down their arms,
made the best of their way. Darius, the instant he saw his left wing broken, was one of
the first who fled in his chariot; but getting
afterwards into craggy rugged places, he
mounted on horseback, throwing down his bow,
shield, and royal mantle. Alexander, however
did not attempt to pursue him, till he saw his
phalanx had conquered the Greeks who ob-
stinately opposed them, and that the Persian
horse were put to flight; which proved of great
advantage to the prince that fled. In this battle, sixty thousand of the Persian infantry, and

ten

ten thousand horsemen, were slain; while of Alexander's army, there fell but two hundred and eighty in all.

Sysigambis, Darius's mother, and that monarch's queen, were found remaining in the camp, with two of the king's daughters, his son, yet a child, and some Persian ladies; for the rest had been carried to Damascus, with part of Darius's treasure, and all such things as contributed only to the luxury and magnificence of his court. No more than three thousand talents were found in his camp; but the rest of the treasure fell afterwards into the hands of Parmenio, at the taking of the city of Damascus.

The next day, Alexander visited his royal prisoners; and his noble and generous behaviour on this occasion, Plutarch occasion to say, that " the princesses of Persia lived in an enemy's camp, as if they had been in some sacred temple, unseen, unapproached, and unmolested." Sysigambis was distinguished by extraordinary marks of Alexander's favours: Darius himself could not have treated her with more respect than did that generous prince. He allowed her to regulate the funerals of all the Persians of the royal family, who had fallen in battle; and, through her intercession, he pardoned several of Darius' nobles, who had justly incurred his displeasure. This magnanimous conduct has done more honour to Alexander's character, than all his splendid conquests. The gentleness of his manners to his suppliant captives, his chastity and continence, when he had the power to enforce obedience, were setting an

example

example to heroes, which it has been the pride of many since to imitate.

After this conquest, all Phœnicia, the capital city Tyre, only excepted, was yielded to the conqueror. Good fortune followed him so fast, that it rewarded him beyond his expectations. Antigonus, his general in Asia, overthrew the Capadocians, Paphlagonians, and others lately revolted. Aristodemus, the Persian admiral was overcome at sea, and a great part of his fleet taken. The city of Damascus, also, in which the treasures of Darius were deposited, was given up to Alexander.

Alexander next went to Sidonia, whose king, Strabo, he dethroned for his attachment to Darius, and permitted Hephæstion to elect in his stead, whomsoever of the Sidonians he should judge worthy of so exalted a character. This favourite was quartered at the house of two brothers, who were young, and of the most considerable family in the city. To these he offered the crown; but they refused it, telling him, that, according to the laws of their country, no person could ascend the throne unless he were of the royal blood. Hephæstion, admiring this greatness of soul, which could contemn what others strive to obtain by fire and sword, "Continue, (said he to them) in this way of thinking, you who seem sensible, that it is much more glorious to refuse than to accept a diadem. However, name me some person of the royal family, who may remember when he be king, that it was you who set the crown on his head." The brothers observing, that several

though

through excessive ambition, aspired to this high station, and to obtain it paid a servile court to Alexander's favourites, declared, that they did not know any person more worthy of the diadem than one Abdolonymus, descended, though at a great distance, from the royal family; but who, at the same time, was so poor that he was obliged to get his bread by day labour in a garden without the city. His honesty and integrity had reduced him, as well as many more, to such extreme poverty. Solely intent upon his labour, he did not hear the clashing of the arms which had shaken all Asia. The two brothers went immediately in search of Abdolonymus, with the royal garment, and found him weeding in his garden. When they saluted him king, Abdolonymus looked upon the whole as a dream; and, unable to guess the meaning of it, asked if they were not ashamed to ridicule him in that manner. But as he made a greater resistance than suited their inclinations, they themselves washed him, and threw over his shoulders a purple robe richly embroidered with gold; then, after repeated oaths of their being in earnest, they conducted him to the palace.

Alexander commanded the new elected prince to be sent for, and, after surveying him attentively a long time, he spoke thus: "Thy air and mein do not contradict what is related of thy extraction; but I should be glad to know with what frame of mind thou didst bear thy poverty." "Would to the gods (replied he) that I may bear this crown with equal patience!—

These

Melampus invested with Royalty.

These hands have procured me all I desired; and whilst I possessed nothing, I wanted nothing." This answer gave Alexander an high idea of Abdolonymus's virtue; so that he presented him, not only with the rich furniture that belonged to Strabo, and part of the Persian plunder, but likewise annexed one of the neighbouring provinces to his dominions.

The Macedonians had already subdued Syria and Phœnicia, the city of Tyre excepted. This city was justly entitled the Queen of the sea, that element bringing to it the tribute of all nations. She boasted of having first invented navigation, and taught mankind the art of braving the winds and waves by the assistance of a frail bark. The happy situation of Tyre, the conveniency and extent of its ports, the character of its inhabitants, who were industrious, laborious, patient, and extremely courteous to strangers, invited thither merchants from all parts of the globe: so that it might be considered, not so much a city belonging to any particular nation, as the common city of all nations, and the centre of their commerce.

Alexander thought it necessary, both for his pride and his interest, to take the city, though it was generally supposed to be impregnable from its fortifications, and inaccessible from its situation. Alexander, however, prepared for the siege, which is one of the most celebrated recorded in history. After a long and obstinate defence on the side of the Tyrians, and a tedious and almost hopeless attack of the besiegers, Alexander took it by storm; and thus fell Tyre, that had been for many ages the most flourishing city in the world, and had spread the arts of commerce into the remotest regions.

CHAP. X.

WHILST Alexander was carrying on the siege of Tyre, he received a second letter from Darius, in which that monarch seemed more sensible of his power than before: he now gave him the title of king, and offered him ten thousand talents, as a ransom for his captive mother, and wife: he offered him his daughter Statira in marriage, with all the country he had conquered, as far as the river Euphrates: he hinted to him the inconstancy of fortune, and described at large the powers he was still possessed of to oppose.

These terms were so considerable, that, when the king debated upon them in council, Parmenio, one of his generals, could not help observing, that, if he were Alexander, he would agree to such a proposal. To which Alexander nobly replied, "And so would I, were I Parmenio." He therefore treated the proposal of Darius with haughty contempt, and refused to accept of treasures which he already conceived as his own.

From Tyre, Alexander marched to Jerusalem where the Jews opened their gates to receive him. From this city, he went on to Gaza, where he found a more obstinate resistance than

he had expected; but at length, taking the town
by storm, and having cut the garrison, consisting of ten thousand men, to pieces, with brutal
ferocity, he ordered Bœtis, the governor, to be
brought before him; and having in vain endeavoured to intimidate him, commanded, at last,
that holes should be bored through his heels,
and thus to be tied by cords to the back of his
chariot, and in this manner to be dragged
round the walls of the city. This he did in
imitation of Achilles, whom Homer describes
as having dragged Hector round the walls of
Troy in the same manner: but it was reading that poet to very little advantage, to imitate
this hero in the most unworthy part of his character.

He then marched into Egypt, and possessed
himself of the whole of it, without meeting
with the least opposition. He afterwards visited
the temple of Jupiter, and caused himself
to be acknowledged by the priests as the son of
that god. Having settled his affairs in Egypt,
he set out to march against Darius, who was
now preparing to oppose him.

On his march, Statira, the wife of Darius,
died in child-bed, and was honoured with a
funeral ceremony due to her exalted character
and station. The news of that melancholy
event was carried to Darius by Tricus, one of
Statira's eunuchs, who had affected his escape
from the Macedonian camp. The news of
Statira's death overwhelmed the mind of Darius
with the deepest sorrow; but when he was told
of the generous manner, in which the royal
captives

captives had been treated, he broke out into this exclamation: " Ye gods, the guardians of our births, and who decree the fate of nations, grant that I may be enabled to leave the Persian state rich and flourishing, as I found it; that I may have it in my power to make Alexander a proper return for his generosity to the dearest pledges of my affection! But, if the duration of this empire is near at an end, and the greatness of Persia about to be forgotten, may none but Alexander be permitted to sit on the throne of Cyrus! Such sentiments in a despotic prince must give a very favourable idea of the liberality of his mind.

The armies of Alexander and Darius were now hastily approaching each other, and at length met on a plain near the city of Arbela. The army of Darius, consisted, at least, of six hundred thousand foot, and forty thousand horse; and the other of no more than forty thousand foot, and about eight thousand horse. The two armies engaged, and the battle was obstinate and bloody; but the Persians were at length routed, and Darius and his army put to flight. Alexander then marched for Babylon, and entered that city in triumph, being received by its inhabitants in the most magnificent manner. He next took possession of Perepolis, at the head of his victorious soldiers; who, though the inhabitants made no resistance, began to cut in pieces all those who still remained in the city. However, the king soon put an end to the massacre, and forbad his soldiers to commit

While Alexander was thus triumphing in all the exultation of succefs, the wretched Darius was by this time arrived at Ecbatana, the capital of Media. There remained still with this fugitive prince thirty thoufand foot; among whom were four thoufand Greeks, who were faithful to him to the laft. Befides thefe he had four thoufand flingers, and upwards of three thoufand Bactrian horfe, whom Beffus, their governor, commanded. Darius, even with fo fmall a force, ftill conceived hopes of oppofing his rival, or at leaft of protracting the war; but he was furrounded with traitors, his want of fuccefs having turned all mankind againft him. Nabarzanes, one of the greateft lords of Perfia, and general of the horfe, had confpired with Beffus, general of the Bactrians, to commit the blackeft of all crimes: to feize upon the perfon of the king, and lay him in chains, which they might eafily do, as each of them had a great number of foldiers under his command. Their defign was, if Alexander fhould purfue them, to fecure themfelves by giving up Darius alive into his hands; and, in cafe they efcaped, to murder that prince, and afterwards ufurp his crown, and begin a new war. Thefe traitors foon won over the troops, by reprefenting to them, that they were going to their deftruction; that they would foon be crufhed under the ruin of an empire, which was juft ready to fall; at the fame time that Bactriana was open to them, and offered them immenfe rifhes. Thefe promifes foon prevailed upon the perfidious army;

the

the Greek mercenaries excepted, who rejected all their proposals with disdain. Darius, thus betrayed by his generals, and pursued by his enemies, the Greeks solicited the honour of protecting his person, assuring him they would so do, at the expence of the last drop of their blood. But his noble spirit would not suffer him to accept the offer: "If my own subjects (said he) will not give me protection, how can I submit to receive it from the hands of strangers?" His faithful Grecian soldiers, finding it beyond their power to grant him any relief, threw themselves upon the mercy of Alexander; who, in consideration of their noble spirit, forgave them, and employed them in his own service.

The traitors seized and bound their monarch in chains of gold, under the appearance of honour, as he was a king; then enclosing him in a covered chariot, they set out towards Bactriana. In this manner they carried him with the utmost dispatch; until being informed, that the Grecian army was still closely pursuing them, they found it impossible either to conciliate the friendship of Alexander, or to secure a throne for themselves. They, therefore once more gave Darius his liberty, and desired him to make the best of his escape with them from the conqueror; but he replied that the gods were ready to revenge the evils he had already suffered; and, appealing to Alexander for justice, refused to follow a band of traitors. At these words they fell into the utmost fury, wounding him with their darts and

their

their spears, and left him to linger in this manner, unattended, the remainder of his wretched life. The traitors then made their escape different ways; while the victorious Macedonians at length coming up, found Darius in solitude, lying in his chariot, and drawing near his end. However, he had strength enough, before he died, to call for drink, which a Macedonian, Polystratus by name, brought him. On this melancholy occasion, the generosity of the unfortunate monarch shone forth, in the address he made to this stranger: " Now, indeed, (said he) I suffer the extremity of misery, since it is not in my power to reward thee for this act of humanity." He had a Persian prisoner, whom he employed as his interpreter. Darius, after drinking the liquor that had been given him, turned to the Macedonian, and told him, that in the deplorable state to which he was reduced, he however should have the comfort to speak to one who could understand him, and that his last words would not be lost. He therefore charged him to tell Alexander, that he had died in his debt, that he gave him many thanks, for the great humanity he had exercised towards his mother, his wife, and his children, whose lives he had not only spared, but restored to their former splendour; that he besought the gods to give victory to his arms, and make him monarch of the universe; that he thought he need not entreat him to revenge the execrable murder committed on his person, as that was the common cause of kings.

After

After this, taking Polystratus by the hand, "Give him (said he) thy hand, as I give thee mine; and carry him, in my name, the only pledge I am able to give of my gratitude and affection." Having said these words, he breathed his last.

Alexander coming up a moment after, and seeing Darius's body, he wept bitterly; and, by the strongest testimonies of affection that could be given, proved how intimately he was affected with the unhappiness of a prince who deserved better. He immediately pulled off his military cloak, and threw it on Darius's body; then causing it to be embalmed, and his coffin to be adorned with royal magnificence, he sent it to Sysigambis, to be interred with the honours usually paid to the deceased Persian monarchs, and entombed with his ancestors. Thus died Darius, in the fiftieth year of his age, six of which he reigned with felicity. In him the Persian empire ended, after having existed from the time of Cyrus the Great, a period of 299 years.

The traitor Bessus did not escape the fate due to his crimes. Alexander pursued him, to avenge on the murderer the death of his royal master. After wandering, in anxiety and horror, from province to province, he was delivered, by the associates of his guilt, into the hands of Alexander, by whom he was put to a cruel death.

CHAP.

CHAP. XI.

THE death of Darius only served to enflame the spirit of ambition in Alexander to pursue further conquests. He crossed Parthia, and arrived in the province of Hyrcania, which submitted to his arms. He afterwards subdued the Mandii, the Arii, the Drangæ, the Hrachosii, and several other nations, into which his army marched with greater speed than people generally travel. He frequently would pursue an enemy for whole days and nights together, almost without suffering his troops to take any rest. By this prodigious rapidity, he came unawares upon nations, who thought him at a great distance, and subdued them before they had time to put themselves in a posture of defence.

Alexander, now enjoying a little repose, abandoned himself to sensuality; and he, whom the arms of the Persians could not conquer, fell a victim to their vices. Nothing was now to be seen but games, parties of pleasure, women and excessive fasting, in which he used to revel whole days and nights. Not satisfied with the buffoons, and the performers on instrumental music, whom he had brought with him out of Greece, he obliged the captive women, whom he carried along with him, to sing songs after the manner of their country. He happened, among those women, to perceive

one who appeared in deeper affliction than the
rest, and who by a modest, and at the same
time a noble confusion, discovered a greater
reluctance than the others to appear in public.
She was a perfect beauty, which was very
much heightened by her bashfulness, whilst she
threw her eyes to the ground, and did all in
her power to conceal her face. The king soon
imagined, by her air and mien, that she was
not of vulgar birth; and enquiring himself into it, the lady answered, that she was grand-
daughter to Ochus, who not long before had
swayed the Persian scepter, and daughter of
his son; that she had married Hystaspes, who
was related to Darius, and general of a great
army. Alexander, being touched with compassion, when he heard the unhappy fate of a
princess of the blood royal, and the sad condition to which she was reduced, not only gave
her liberty, but returned all her possessions;
and caused her husband to be sought for, in
order that she might be restored to him. This
single act of generosity should draw a veil over
many of his faults.

Hitherto we have seen Alexander triumphing
by a course of virtue, we are now to behold
him swollen up by success, spoiled by flattery,
and enervated by vices, exhibiting a very doubtful character, and mixing the tyrant with the
hero. Upon a charge of a real or imaginary
plot against him, he first put Philotas to death,
and afterwards the father, Parmenio, who was
at the time of his death seventy years of age,

and

and had served his master with fidelity and zeal, which in the end was thus rewarded. Alexander, thus uniting in his person at once great cruelty and great enterprize, still marched forward in search of new nations, whom he might subdue.

Having subdued the Massagetæ, the Dahæ, and other nations, he entered the province of Barsaria, from thence he advanced to Maracander, and appointed Clitus governor of that province. This was an old officer, who had fought under Philip, and signalized himself on many occasions. At the battle of the Grannicus, as Alexander was fighting bareheaded, and Rasaces had his arm raised, in order to strike him behind, Clitus covered the king with his shield, and cut off the barbarian's hand.— This favour, however, only advanced Clitus to a post of greater danger. One evening, at an entertainment, the king, after drinking immoderately, began to celebrate his own exploits, in a manner which shocked all his old generals. Clitus, who was also intoxicated, contradicted Alexander in all his assertions, and sung, with an air of insolence, verses reflecting highly on the price, who seeing the general near him, he struck him dead with a javelin. The king had no sooner murdered his faithful servant, than he perceived the atrociousness of the act; he threw himself upon the dead body, forced out the javelin, and would have destroyed himself, had he not been prevented by his guards, who seized and carried him forcibly to his own a-

partment

apartment, where the flattery and perfuasions of his friends at length served to alleviate his remorse. Alexander, in order to divert his melancholy, assembled his army, and marched in pursuit of new conquests.

He advanced into India, which having never been a warlike nation, he subdued it with the rapidity rather of a traveller than a conqueror. Numberless petty states submitted to him, sensible that his stay would be short, and his conquests evanescent. Sailing down the river Indus, and conquering every thing in his way, he at last come to the country of the Oxydraci and the Mallis, the most valiant people in the East. However, Alexander defeated them in several engagements, dispossessing them of their strong holds, and at last marched against their capital city, where the greatest part of their forces were retired. It was upon this occasion, that seizing a scaling ladder, himself first mounted the wall, followed only by two of his officers. His attendants believing him to be in danger, mounted swiftly to succour him; but the ladder breaking, he was left alone. It was now that his rashness became his safety; for leaping from the wall into the city, which was crowded with enemies, sword in hand, he repulsed such as were nearest, and even killed the general, who advanced in the throng. Thus with his back to a tree that happened to be near, he received all the darts of the enemy in a shield, and kept even the boldest at a distance. At last, an Indian discharging an arrow of three feet

long

long, it pierced his coat of mail and his right breast, and so great a quantity of blood issued from the wound, that he dropped his arms, and lay as dead. The Indian came to strip him, supposing him really what he appeared; but Alexander that instant recalled his spirits, and plunged a dagger in his side. By this time, a part of the king's attendants came to his succour, and forming themselves round his body, till his soldiers without found means of bursting the gates, saved him, and put all the inhabitants, without distinction, to the sword.

The wound which at first seemed dangerous, having, in the space of six or seven days, assumed a more favourable appearance, Alexander mounted his horse, and shewed himself to the army, who seemed to view him with insatiable pleasure. Then continuing his voyage, and subduing the country on each side, as he passed along, the pilots perceived from the swell of the river, that the sea could not be far distant; and they informed the king, that they already felt the breezes of the ocean. Nothing so much astonished the Macedonian soldiers as the ebbing and flowing of the tide. Accustomed to the gentle floods of the Mediterranean, they were amazed when they saw the Indus rise to a great heighth, and overflow the country, which they considered as a mark of divine resentment. They were no less terrified some hours afterwards, when they saw the river forsake its banks, and leave those lands uncovered, which it had so lately overflowed. Thus,

after

after a voyage of nine months, he at last stood upon the shore; and after having offered sacrifices to Neptune, and looked wishfully on the immense expanse of waters before him, he is said to have wept for having no more worlds left to conquer. Here he put an end to his excursions; and, having appointed Nearchus admiral of his fleet, with orders to coast along the Indian shore as far as the Persian gulf, he set out with his army for Babylon.

His army sustained incredible hardships on their return: passing through a country destitute of all sorts of provisions, they were obliged to feast on the beasts of burden, and were forced to burn those rich spoils, for the sake of which they had encountered so many dangers. Those diseases also, that generally accompany famine, compleated their calamity, and destroyed them in great numbers: but the king's fortitude appeared to great advantage on this occasion. The army being in absolute want of water, some soldiers were sent to endeavor to find out a spring. They fortunetely fell upon one; but it yielded them but a very small quantity of water. With what they had gotten, the soldiers returned rejoicing to the king, who, instead of drinking it, poured it upon the ground, unwilling that his soldiers should sustain a calamity, in which he refused to bear a part. This generous act inspired the soldiery with fresh spirits.

After a march of sixty days, they arrived in the province of Gedrosia, the fertility of which soon banished from the minds of the soldiery all their former difficulties. Alexander passed through the country, not in the military pomp of a conqueror, but in the licentious disguise of an enthusiast: still willing to imitate Bacchus, he was drawn by eight horses, on a scaffold in the form of a square stage, where he spent the days and nights in feasting. Along the roads where he passed, were placed casks of wine in great abundance, and these the soldiers drained in honour of their mock deity. The whole country echoed with the sound of instruments, and the howling of bacchanals, who, with their hair dishevelled, and frantic mirth, ran up and down, abandoning themselves to every kind of lewdness. This vice produced one of a much more formidable nature in the king's mind; for it always inflamed his passions to cruelty, and the executioner generally crowned the feast.

After various combats, conquests, cruelties, follies, and excesses, Alexander arrived at Babylon. On his approach to the city, many sinister omens were observed; on which account the Chaldeans, who pretended to foresee future events, attempted to persuade him not to enter that city. The Greek philosophers, on the other hand, displayed the futility of their predictions. Babylon was a theatre for him to display his glory on; and ambassadors from all the nations he had conquered were there in readiness to celebrate his triumphs. After making a most magnificent entry, he gave audience to the ambassadors with a grandeur and dignity suitable to his power, yet with the affability and politeness of a private courtier.

Alexander, finding Babylon, in extent and conveniency superior to all other cities of the East, he resolved to make it the seat of his empire; and for that purpose was desirable of adding to it all the ornaments possible. Though he was much employed in projects of this kind, and in schemes beyond human power to execute, he spent the greater part of his time in such pleasures as this magnificent city afforded; but his pleasures often terminated in licentiousness and riot. The recollection of the cruel manner, in which he had put a period to the lives of some of his best friends and favourites festered in his mind, and cast a thick gloom over his spirits; to dissipate which, required the application of some very powerful remedy. The remedy, to which he had recourse, was *intemperance*. He was, of course frequently invited to banquets, at which he drank so immoderately, as often to have no command left of himself.

On a particular occasion, having spent the whole night in a debauch, a second was proposed: he accepted the invitation, and drank to such excess, that he fell upon the floor, to appearance dead, and in this lifeless manner was carried, a sad spectacle of debauchery, to his palace. The fever continued, with some intervals, in which he gave the necessary orders for the sailing of the fleet, and the marching of his land forces, being perſuaded he ſhoud ſoon recover. But at laſt, finding himſelf paſt hopes, and his voice beginning to fail, he gave his ring to Perdiccas, with orders to convey his corps to the temple of Ammon. He ſtruggled, however, with death for ſome time, and raiſing himſelf upon his elbow, he gave his hand to the ſoldiers, who preſſed to kiſs it. Being then aſked to whom he would leave his empire, he anſwered, " To the moſt worthy." Perdiccas enquiring at what time he ſhould pay him divine honours, he replied, " When you are happy." With theſe words he expired, being thirty-two years and eight months old, of which he had reigned twelve, with more fortune than virtue.

By the death of this illuſtrious conqueror were fulfilled many of the prophecies of the ſacred writers. One of them is ſingularly ſtriking: " The temple of Belus ſhall be broken down to the ground, never to raiſe from its ruins." That the word of God might ſtand firm, Alexander is cut off, at the very inſtant he is preparing to rebuild that temple, and to raiſe Babylon to its wanted ſplendour. Alexander left one ſon, named Hercules, who was born of Barſine, the daughter of Artabazus, and widow of Memnon. Both Roxana and Statira are ſaid to have been left pregnant.

In whatever light we view this monarch, we ſhall find little to admire, and leſs to imitate. That courage, for which he was celebrated, is but a ſubordinate virtue; that fortune, which constantly attended him, was but an accidental advantage; that discipline, which prevailed in his army, was produced and cultivated by his father; but his intemperance, his cruelty, his vanity, his passion for useless conquests, were all his own. His victories, however, served to crown the pyramid of Grecian glory; they served to show, to what a degree the arts of peace can promote those of war. In this picture, we view a combination of petty states, by the arts of refinement, growing more than a match for the rest of the world united, and leaving mankind an example of the superiority of intellect over brutal force.

CHAP. XII.

ALEXANDER having, by his last words, bequeathed his empire "to the most worthy," men who had been accustomed to rule with absolute power, in distant, extensive, populous, and wealthy provinces, must have been highly pleased to find, that their sovereign's will threw no bar in their way to dominion or power. There was one, however, who appeared to have an extraordinary claim to distinction: Perdiccas, to whom Alexander, in his last moments, had delivered his royal signet. Possessed of merit, equal at least to that of his competitors, this adventitious circumstance might seem to have given him a superior title to the vast object in question; but his rivals were too proud to suffer an equal to be exalted above them, without throwing some embarrassment in his way; and too fond of power to bestow a title to an empire, without advancing their own pretensions. Accordingly they all remonstrated, and opposed Perdicca's elevation; and, finding that they were not likely to succeed in their private schemes, by acting interestedly, they resolved to overturn his, by acting justly, in supporting the claims of the lawful heirs to the crown. These were Hercules, the son of Alexander; and Aridæus, Alexander's own brother. There was little or no contest about Aridæus's right to a share in the sovereignty. He had been acknowledged to be insane; and that circumstance, perhaps more than his consanguinity to the king, procured him an easy admission to the throne. The right of Hercules was not so readily recognized: his mother was not of royal extraction; and as Alexander had always shewn a preference to Roxana and Statira, and had, moreover, omitted to mention Hercules in his last hours, his title was at once set aside; but the exclusive right to the throne was not to be granted to one person. It was therefore judged proper, by all the leading men, to divide the sovereignty between Aridæus and the child to be born of Roxana, should it prove a son. This appointment was easily acceded to, as the government that was naturally to be expected from it, would have full scope for the exercise of avarice and ambition.

tion. This settlement being made, the various competitors for the Macedonian empire retired to their respective employments.

Roxana being delivered of a son, whom they named Alexander, Olympias had been recalled to take charge of her infant grandson, and to sanction the new administration of Macedon by her presence. On her arrival at Macedon, she first let lose her savage revenge on Aridæus, and his queen Eurydice. Aridæus, the son of Philip by a concubine had from his infancy been subjected to that aversion and hatred from Olympias, which the relationship that subsisted between her and him naturally excited. The infirmity of his understanding was said to have been the effect of a potion, which she gave him. Cynane, the mother of Aridæus' queen, had been murdered at the instigation of Olympias. Amyntas, her father, the son of Philip the First's elder brother, had also been destroyed through her contrivance : so that neither Aridæus, nor Eurydice his wife, could be supposed to look upon her with complacence. Indeed, they had every reason to apprehend bad consequences from her getting into power, and they set themselves to provide for the worst. Eurydice raised an army, and marched to meet Olympias ; but on the two armies meeting, the troops of Eurydice went over to the standard of Olympias, and Aridæus and his queen fell into her hands.

Olympias persecuted the royal couple with all that unrelenting hatred which marked her disposition : they were confined to a
prison,

prison, which was so small, that they could
scarcely turn themselves in it. Their wretched
sustenance was thrown in at a little hole,
through which passed light and air, and all the
other limitted comforts they were permitted to
enjoy. Perceiving that this barbarous treat-
ment had no other effect than to excite the
compassion of the people, and fearing that
their commiseration would soon be converted
into indignation towards her, she resolved to
put a period to the miserable existence of her
prisoners. She instructed some Thracians to
enter the prison, and dispatch Aridæus, which
they did without remorse. He had reigned six
years and four months.

This inhuman action being perpetrated,
Olympias sent messengers to the queen, furnished with a poinard, a rope, and a cup of
poison, desiring her to choose which she
pleased. They found her binding up the
wounds of her bleeding spouse, with linen
which she had torn from her own body, and
paying all that decent and solemn respect to
the lifeless corse, which became her deplorable
situation. She received the message that was
brought to her with the greatest composure;
and, after entreating the gods, that Olympias
might be rewarded with the like present, she
took the rope, and strangled herself. Thus
were that hapless pair cut off. Olympias had now
set a period to the life of Aridæus, whom she
had long since deprived of every rational enjoyment, by robbing him of his understanding;
and she had completed the ruin of Eurydice

and her family, by consigning her to an end similar to that, which her violent and vindictive passions had formerly procured to her unfortunate parents. Nor was her thirst of blood yet quenched; for he caused Nicanor, the brother of Cassander, to be put to death. The body of Iolas, another brother of Cassander, which had long rested in the tomb, she had brought forth, and exposed on the highway; and an hundred Macedonians of noble birth were seized and executed, on suspicion of having been in the interest of Cassander. At last, however, the fortune of war threw her into the power of Cassander, who delivered her into the hands of those whose kindred she had murdered, and who thereupon cut her throat.

The furious contentions that now subsisted among the ambitious surviving captains of Alexander, deluged Greece in blood, and brought on the most unnatural murders. Besides those horrid and unnatural scenes we have already described, Roxana and her son Alexander were imprisoned, and treated with contempt; and Hercules, the son of Alexander by Bartine, the only remaining branch of the royal family, was murdered about two years after. Not more than twenty-eight years had elapsed since the death of Alexander, and not a single branch of his house remained to enjoy a portion of that empire, which Philip and his son had acquired at the price of the greatest policy, dangers, and bloodshed. Such, to the royal family of Macedon, were the effects

Page 147.

Philip sitting in judgment on his own Sons.

of that ambition, which had lighted the torch of war over Europe, Asia, and Africa.

Among the last kings of Macedon, was Philip, son of Demetrius. He had two sons, Perseus and Demetrius; the former of which accused the latter of a design to assassinate the king, who retiring into the inner apartment of his palace, with two of his nobles, sat in solemn judgment on his two sons, being under the agonizing necessity, whether the charge should be proved or disapproved, of finding one of them guilty. Perseus took care to procure such evidence against his brother, as might not fail of convicting him, and Demetrius was accordingly put to death. Philip, when too late, discovered that he had been imposed upon by a forgery, and died of a broken heart. He was succeeded by his son Perseus, who, some time after, was taken prisoner by the Romans, led in triumph through the streets of Rome, and then thrown into a dungeon, where he starved himself to death.

The fatal dissention among the Grecian chiefs exposed them to the inroads of every neighbouring power. The Romans, after the defeat of Perseus, established a new form of government in Macedon. The whole kingdom was divided into four districts; the inhabitants of each were to have no connection, intermarriage, or exchange of possessions, with those of the other districts; and, among other regulations tending to reduce them to a state of the most abject slavery, they were inhibited from the use of arms, unless in such places as

were

were exposed to the incursions of the barbarians. Triumphal games at Amphipolis, to which all the neighbouring nations, both Europeans and Asiatics, were invited, announced the extended dominion of Rome, and the humiliation not only of Macedon, but of all Greece; for the Romans now found nothing in that part of the world that was able to oppose them.

Greece, now sunk in that mass of nations which composed the Roman empire, had lost every vestige of national existence; and, while she was excluded from all participation in the prosperity of her conquerors, she shared deeply in her misfortunes. The civil wars of Rome drenched Greece with blood; and, when that war was concluded, whoever had not appeared on the side of the victor, was considered as his enemy. Greece, in common with the other Roman provinces, had suffered many oppressions under the emperors, and from the repeated invasions of barbarians, when the accession of Constantine the Great to the Imperial throne, seemed to promise to the Grecian annals a new æra of glory, and some comforts for their past misfortunes.

The hopes of Greece, however, were even here disappointed; for Constantine, by dividing his dominions among his three sons, involved the empire in the flames of civil war; and his son Julian, who at last prevailed, overturned every thing his father had done. He was unable to protect the public prosperity, undermined by the despotism of a military government, and a
general

general pusillanimity of manners. These invited attacks on the empire on every side. Julian was forced to yield a considerable territory to the Persian monarch. In Britain, the Roman ramparts were opposed in vain to the hardy valour of the north; even the legionary troops had been found unable to sustain the shocks of the unconquered Caledonians. The German tribes renewed their inroads into Gaul; Africa rebelled, and a spirit of discontent and insurrection began to appear among the barbarian tribes on the Danube. In the reign of the Emperor Valens, the Huns, a new tribe of barbarians, in manners and aspect more horrid than any that had yet appeared on the Roman frontiers, plundered and drove from their settlements the Gothic tribes on the further side of the Danube. Gratian, nephew and heir to Valens, shared the empire with Theodosius, whom the calamities of the times raised to the possession of the whole. The abilities and personal valour of this prince bestowed on the empire an appearance of vigour during his reign; but his sons Arcadius and Honorius, between whom he divided the empire, brought up in the bosom of a luxurious palace, and sunk in effeminacy, were unequal to the task of governing an empire weakened by division. The reign of Honorius concluded the Roman empire in the East. Alaric, the Gothic chief, who, twenty-five years before, deemed it an honour to bear arms on the side of the empire, was adorned with the imperial purple. Augustulus, the last Roman who was graced with imperial dignity at Rome, was compelled to abdicate the Western empire by Odoacer, king of the Heruli, about the year of Christ 475.

Amidst the calamities which attended and followed after this revolution, Greece saw her magnificient cities laid in ruins, her numerous towns levelled with the ground, and those monuments of her glory, which had hitherto escaped barbarian outrage, defaced and overthrown; while the wretched descendants of men, who blessed the nations with science and art, were either enslaved by the invaders, or led into captivity, or slaughtered by the swords of barbarians. Without inhabitants, or cultivation, and buried as it were in ruins, Greece was too insignificant to be an object of ambition, and left to the possession of any of the rovers of those days, who chose to make a temporary settlement in that desolated country.—Constantinople itself, during the greater part of this gloomy period, retained little more than a shadow of greatness. The chief inhabitants were those families who, during the incursions of the barbarians, had made their escape to the mountains. Such was the state of Greece, with little variation, from the Gothic invasion, to the final overthrow of the Eastern empire by the Ottoman arms, in the year of the Christian æra one thousand four hundred and fifty-three.

However, even in the midst of war, devastation and slavery, Greece continued long to be the seat of philosophy and the fine arts. Whatever conjectures may be formed concerning the advancement of science in India and

GRECIAN STATES.

in Egypt, it is certain, that Greece was the country which enlightened, exalted, and adorned the rest of Europe, and set an example of whatever is beautiful and great. It was the genius of Greece that formed those very politicians and heroes, who first bent her lofty spirit under the yoke of foreign dominion. It was in Thebes, under the tuition of Epaminondas, that her heroes were trained to a love of glory, and of all those arts and accomplishments of both peace and war, by which it is best attained. It was a Grecian philosopher who taught Alexander how to manage the passions, and govern the minds of men; while the writings of Homer, by a most powerful contagion, infpired his mind with a contempt of danger and death in the pursuit of glory.—As the light of Greece illuminated her Macedonian, fo it fpread over her Roman conquerors. Philofophy, literature, and arts, began to follow glory and empire to Rome in the times of Sylla and Lucullus, and, in their progrefs, drew to different fchools every man of rank and fafhion in Italy. Wealth, luxury, and corruption, and at laft tyranny, banifhed it from Rome; but while it lafted, it made up, in fome degree, for the want of liberty: if it were unable to refift oppreffive power, it fuftained the mind in the midft of fufferings.—Even in the worft of times, when the Roman empire was in the laft period of its decline, amidft the ruins of the ancient world, diftracted by internal divifions, and torn to pieces by the incurfions of barbarous nations

from

from the east, north, and south, a succession of ingenious, learned, and contemplative minds, transmitted the sacred light of truth (which, like the sun, though eclipsed or obscured, never deserts the world) from one age to another.

The modern Greeks, without the least political importance, and sunk in slavery to a military government, retain but little of their original character. The gradations, by which that character faded away, are clearly discernible in their history, and present to the attentive eye a speculation of great curiosity and importance. The relaxation of manners gradually undermined the political institutions of the leading states of Greece, and the complete subversion of these, reacting on manners, accelerated on the declination of virtue. Simplicity, modesty, temperance, sincerity, and good faith, fled first: the last of the virtues that took its flight, was military valour.

CHRO-

CHRONOLOGICAL TABLE

OF THE PRINCIPAL

OCCURRENCES AND EVENTS

DURING THE

EXISTENCE

OF THE

GRECIAN STATES.

N. B. The Figures at the End of the Lines refer to the Date of the Events before the Birth of Christ.

Before J. C.

FOUNDATION of the Kingdom of Athens by Cecrops - - 1556
Foundation of the Kingdom of Lacedemonia - - - 1516
Troy taken by the Greeks - - 1184
Foundation of the City of Thebes 1055
Homer and Hesiod lived about - 844
Foundation of the kingdom of Macedon 794
Beginning of the common æra of the Olympiad 776
Thales of Miletus, founder of the Ionic sect - - - - - 640
Draco, legislator of Athens - 624
Solon, and the other sages of Greece, lived about - - 604

Pythagoras

CHRONOLOGICAL TABLE.

Pythagoras lived about	564
Simonides, the celebrated poet	560
Pisistratus makes himself master of Athens	559
Heraclitus, chief of the sect that bears his name	544
Death of Pisistratus	526
Battle of Marathon	491
Death of Miltiades	490
Xerxes succeeds his father Darius	485
Xerxes sets out to make war against the Greeks	480
Battle of Thermopylae	480
Battle of Salamis, and Xerxes' retreat into Persia	480
Battle of Platea	479
Pindar, the celebrated poet, flourished about	476
Sophocles and Euripides appeared in Greece about	473
Xerxes killed by Artabanus, the captain of his guard	472
The Persians defeated by the Greeks, and their fleet taken, near the mouth of the river Eurymedon	471
Birth of Socrates	470
Birth of Xenophon	450
End of the war between the Greeks and Persians, which had continued fifty-one years	449
Alcibiades appears in the war between the Corinthians and the people of Corcyra	436

Beginning

CHRONOLOGICAL TABLE.

Beginning of the Peloponnesian war, which lasted twenty-seven years	431
A terrible plague raged at Athens	430
Death of Pericles	429
Lysander makes himself master of Athens, and establishes the Thirty Tyrants	404
Death of Socrates	401
Birth of Aristotle, founder of the Peripatetics	384
Birth of Philip, king of Macedon	383
Birth of Demosthenes	382
Battle of Leuctra	370
Battle of Mantinea, and death of Epimanondas	363
Philip ascends the throne of Macedon	360
Birth of Alexander the Great	356
Plato died	348
Philip declared generalissimo of the Greeks	338
Battle of Cheronea, in which Philip defeats the Athenians and Thebans	338
Death of Philip, who is succeeded by his son, Alexander	336
Thebes taken and destroyed by Alexander	335
Battle of the Grannicus, followed with the conquest of almost all Asia Minor	334
Battle of Issus	333
Tyre taken by Alexander	332
Alexander goes to Jerusalem, makes himself master of Gaza, and soon after of all Egypt. Builds the city of Alexandria	332
Battle of Arbela	331
Darius seized and put in chains by Bessus, and soon after assassinated	330

Thaleſtres, queen of the Amazons, pays
    a viſit to Alexander   -   -   330
Beſſus brought to Alexander, and ſoon
    after put to death   -   -   329
Lyſippus, of Sicyon, a famous ſculptor,
    flouriſhed about   -   -   329
Clitus killed by Alexander at a feaſt   328
Alexander's entrance into India   -   327
Alexander, on his return to Babylon, dies
    there, at the age of thirty-two years
    and eight months   -   -   323
Olympias, the mother of Alexander, cau-
    ſes Aridæus, and Eurydice, his wife,
    to be put to death, as ſhe herſelf is ſoon
    after, by order of Caſſander   317
Greece reduced into a Roman province, un-
    der the name of the province of Achia 146

FINIS.

www.ingramcontent.com/pod-product-compliance
Lightning Source LLC
Chambersburg PA
CBHW030319170426
43202CB00009B/1071